WAR
IN FOCUS

CARLTON
BOOKS

THIS IS A CARLTON BOOK

Published by Carlton Books Limited 2005
A division of the Carlton Publishing Group
20 Mortimer Street
London
WIT 3JW

ISBN 1 84442 557 6

A CIP catalogue for this book is available from the British Library.

Executive Editor: Stella Caldwell
Design: Anita Ruddell
Picture Research: Steve Behan
Production: Lisa Moore

Printed and bound in Dubai

WAR IN FOCUS

PAUL BREWER

CONTENTS

INTRODUCTION
6–15

THE FIRST IMAGES
16–25

THE AMERICAN CIVIL WAR
26–49

IMPERIAL ADVENTURES
50–69

WARS BETWEEN THE GREAT POWERS
70–89

THE FIRST WORLD WAR
90–149

THE INTERWAR YEARS
150–169

THE SECOND WORLD WAR
170–271

THE END OF EMPIRES
272–289

THE COLD WARS
290–301

VIETNAM
302–337

THE MIDDLE EAST
338–369

A WORLD AT WAR
370–383

TERRORISM
384–397

INDEX
398–399

CREDITS
400

INTRODUCTION

"Everyone's saying we're for it. I don't know what to think really. Seems so silly, somehow, all this drill and training if we never go into action."

"I shouldn't worry. There'll be plenty enough for everyone in time."

"Oh, I don't want much you know. Just enough to say I'd been in it."

Brideshead Revisited, EVELYN WAUGH

This conversation between Lieutenant Hooper and Captain Charles Ryde from Evelyn Waugh's novel *Brideshead Revisited*, fictitious though it is, accurately reflects a mood among those who are training for war. Every soldier, sailor, or airman wants to have enough of it, but not too much – and to live to tell the tale, so to speak.

"Action" is the euphemism used by Hooper and there have been several slang terms for combat used by soldiers over the years. "Seeing the elephant" was borrowed by soldiers of the American Civil War from the slang of the California Gold Rush of 1849 to describe the fighting. What would be understood by such a term? It expressed the fact that combat was the most extraordinary and unusual thing imaginable, much like seeing an elephant in the 1840s.

Prior to the invention of the camera, a visual understanding of what war looked like was hard to come by. There have been detailed written descriptions of combat dating back to the Ancient Greeks. Lyric poets in the sixth century BC described the sensations experienced by soldiers fighting in phalanxes. But visual representations were more difficult. Vase paintings for the most part show single combat. A dying man may sag to the ground, but the poet's description of him clutching his entrails, presumably about to spill out, is absent. Sculpture can show blood, as in the famous Dying Gaul, but the wounds remain neat and clean.

Later visual representations could do little better. Painting was expensive and tended to focus on the commanders or on massed formations of troops. War itself became associated with the world of the upper-class duel. A "passage of arms" between knights or dashing fellows in colourful uniforms was the ideal of war, and glory became linked to the concept of battle.

LEFT
Robert Capa during the Spanish Civil War. A legend in war photography, Robert Capa is reported to have once said "If your pictures aren't good enough, you aren't close enough." He died on an Indochina battlefield in 1954.

People still wrote of the awfulness of battle injuries and described the ever-present sensation of fear. But this literature rarely made its way to a wide audience.

Frankly, Lieutenant Hooper has not got the slightest notion of what awaits him on the battlefield. The book is vague about dates, but one can assume that Hooper and his platoon are about to take part in the Allied invasion of Western Europe that began on 6 June 1944. Hooper will then at last have his "action" and may survive to say he had been in it.

War, Hooper will have found, is perhaps the most humiliating experience known to humans. Fear can strip men of their dignity in a second, reducing them to stuttering inarticulacy. It can cause them to foul themselves, a phenomenon noted in the comedies of Aristophanes in the late fifth century BC.

The source of this fear, beyond the potential for the abrupt cessation of all one knows, is the utter savagery of the wounding. A sword blow can remove a nose, sever limbs or rip open the flesh. A bounding cannon ball can shatter limbs or remove foot or head. A shell explosion can do all this and more. High-speed bullets can make a small entry hole and a huge exit wound – one moment, a man was there; the next moment he was a corpse, or perhaps scattered around the ground in pieces.

The experience of war is terrible beyond the imagination of any decent person. However, the invention of the camera and its gradual technical development have done much to show those who, like Hooper, might wonder about getting into action, just what they could be letting themselves in for.

The birth of the camera coincided with the most rapid era of change in the history of warfare, as the Industrial Revolution took hold, first in Europe, and then spread around the world, transmitted in part by the superior weapons of the great colonial empires. Industrial and scientific developments made new weapons possible and government contracts for weapons soon became highly profitable arrangements for industrial concerns. The concept of interchangeable parts in manufactured products was developed to help the production of firearms by Honoré le Blanc in France in the late 18th century. It was further encouraged in the United States by Thomas Jefferson, who had been introduced to the idea while serving as United States ambassador to France. The Springfield Armory, at Springfield, Massachusetts, was one of the first to put this idea into practice. Assembly-line methods were developed in the first decade of the nineteenth century at the Portsmouth Naval Dockyard to equip ships with pulleys, a piece of technology widely used in sailing ships. After the Wright brothers solved the problem of heavier-than-air flight, one of the first markets they sought to exploit was the military one. Wars soon became periods of theoretical and practical industrial developments in which ideas were rapidly refined.

The first war extensively photographed, the Crimean War of 1853–1856, was fought by commanders who still retained an operational and tactical mindset stuck in the Napoleonic Wars some 50 years earlier. Yet technical developments, particularly in the war at sea, were already resulting in important changes. In 1822, a French army officer, Henri Paixhans, designed a shell-firing gun. He suggested that a wooden warship would be extremely vulnerable to shell-fire. An exploding projectile would be particularly effective against a wooden ship, where the explosive effect could start fires more quickly than traditional solid shot. Thirty years later, the first practical demonstration of his theory was provided by the Russian victory over the Turkish fleet at Sinope in November 1853. Although early shells were unreliable, and even at Sinope the results of Russian gunnery were not much faster than could have been achieved by solid shot, the threat of continued improvements led to a search for some counter to the power of the new projectiles. That improvement came with the creation of armoured ships. The French first designed armoured floating batteries to be used in operations against Russian fortresses in the Black Sea, and then extended the idea to a proper sea-going ship, *La Gloire*, launched in 1859.

This rapid move and counter-move pattern of technological change in military and naval affairs is a new historical development, and the one constant of warfare in the era of photography. It explains why the Napoleonic-style uniforms of the first chapter give way, as one turns the pages, to camouflage battledress. It also explains why the close formations of a hundred or so shown in photos taken during the Crimean and American Civil wars are transformed into small groups of four or six in more modern combats.

The technical developments focus on one dialectic that has recurred in warfare throughout history. How does one find the enemy and, once found, kill him? How does one hide from the enemy until one is ready to kill him?

The massed formations of the first chapters reflect the practical mathematics of musketry. Given a certain number of bullets fired at a target, statistically a certain percentage ought to hit. The effect of more advanced small arms technology, including improvements to both bullet propellants and rates of fire brought about in particular by the advent of the machine gun, is simply a matter of putting more bullets into the target area. More bullets equals more hits. Fewer soldiers are needed to fire the same number of bullets at the target. The same calculation is involved with artillery, where quick-firing guns such as the famous French 75mm field gun could be aimed and fired with greater rapidity. More shells in less time equals a need for fewer guns. The automatic shell-loaders of more modern pieces take a further step in this direction by increasing rates of fire still more.

But the paradox is that as rates of fire increase, fewer soldiers are needed. Furthermore, the enthusiasm of soldiers for fighting can be increased by reducing their risk of getting killed. So, since fewer soldiers are needed to deliver the same volume of fire, why not scatter them more widely? And so comes the next stage of the equation. With fewer targets to aim at, more bullets or more explosive power are needed to be sure of hits. And so on.

This, fundamentally, describes the technological problem of warfare. Every other significant development has been an attempt to solve some part of that equation. The aeroplane enabled the enemy to be located from a great height. The submarine allowed the hiding of a ship from view. The atom bomb delivered maximum explosive power over a large area. Of course, reducing warfare to the equivalent of an engineering problem has the unwelcome effect of dehumanizing it. Military vocabulary is full of euphemisms to describe dead people: "casualties", "body count", "rates of attrition". The numbers used by warfare's statisticians to fill in the blanks after these words represent people who have a life that has been brought to an abrupt end. The camera has had the effect of making these people seem more real. During the American Civil War, it was the fashion for those setting out for the fighting to have their portrait taken, normally in uniform, with guns, swords and other martial equipment prominently visible. We can put names to many of these photographs, and today's fascination with tracing family trees means that the forebears and descendants of many of these people can be traced. Suddenly, the history of these men, who may have perished in the conflict, becomes more easily known and consequently more real than a mere series of descriptive statements about a unit's movements from one place to another on the battlefield of Gettysburg.

More importantly, the photograph has – especially since the 1960s – underlined the sheer misery that war causes, and not just to those who fight. It was universally accepted by combat infantrymen in the US Army in the Second World War that there were only three ways out of front-line service. First, for the war to end, which in early June 1944 might have seemed a long way off. Second, to be wounded, although a minor wound would see a soldier back in the front line within weeks or at best months. A major wound could maim for life, not something to be welcomed. Third, to be killed. This equation, more human than the engineering problem of finding and killing, makes grim reading. It also led to a change in the way the US Army fought. During the Vietnam War, there was a time limit beyond which no one would be asked to serve. Make it through a year, and one could get away.

But war has always put civilians in the front line. An army on the march has to move through countryside populated by people. Armed men trained to kill other people can pretty well take whatever they want; who is going to argue? Modern warfare, moreover, has a tendency to enter periods of stasis, when the two forces cannot overcome one another, but remain in roughly the same place for weeks at a time. In such circumstances, civilians find themselves looking at the American combat infantryman's equation, and probably without access to the military medical support that can save the life of even a badly wounded person.

Normandy, in 1944, was a huge battleground. The region's great dairy herd was destroyed by the variety of weapons that pummelled the ground. The sight of dead cows was one of the lasting memories held by those who fought there. As the Germans attempted to escape after the American break-out threatened to trap them in the Falaise Pocket, the pocket itself became a free-fire zone for Allied aircraft. The poor civilians who found themselves trapped in that region are to be pitied. Together with dead cows, dead civilians in the Falaise Pocket provided another unwelcome memory

RIGHT
A Cecil Beaton photograph taken in the Arakan in January 1944, shows a Gurkha carrying a wounded comrade. Beaton was the official photographer for various British government agencies during the Second World War.

to survivors. Finally, and again in connection with the Normandy campaign, one must cast a sorrowful glance in the direction of the Pas de Calais. The Germans believed that the main Allied blow would fall there. The Allies wished them to believe this. In order to fool the Germans, a considerable number of air attacks were launched on the region. Many civilians died, in order that a fiction might be believed.

At least France was a combatant nation in the Second World War in Europe. Worse luck befell those further abroad for whom the war had little relevance. The First World War offers perhaps the most tragic examples, as one wonders how significant the control of German East Africa or German South-West Africa might have seemed to the African peoples living there. During the Second World War, thousands of Burmese fled the Japanese invasion, even though the Japanese promoted an image of themselves as an Asian people seeking to liberate other Asians from European oppression. Some of those Burmese who fled may have had some kind of stake in British rule over the country. Others may just have been afraid of a Japanese Army that had behaved with terrific cruelty in China during the previous five years. Whatever the impulse to flee, the difficult climate and terrain of Burma, together with the lack of any institutional support for refugees, led to many deaths. Even worse was the great famine in Bengal during 1943–1944, largely a consequence of the war, although an already difficult situation was aggravated by a hurricane in October 1942. Between four and five million people died as a direct consequence of policies adopted by the British administrators in India in order to cope with the possibility of a Japanese invasion from Burma.

Inflicting hardship on "enemy" civilians in wartime is often a strategy adopted by one side in the pursuit of victory. The mass bombing inflicted on many countries during the Second World War, including the notorious Dresden raids of February 1945, was not intended to kill civilians. The official targets of such raids were in fact strategically significant objectives such as factories producing war-related materiel, electrical power generators or transmission devices, railway yards and similar sorts of economic targets. However, these targets were industrial ones, and required workers to run them. And those workers tended to live nearby. Furthermore, for all the pre-war talk of precision bombing, practice illustrated that bombers could not be too precise without taking inordinately high casualties. The consequence was that bombs were dropped with the minimum possible risk to the crews of the aeroplanes, but without regard to the risk to civilians. Thus, death tolls such as 50,000 at Hamburg or 80,000 in Tokyo resulted. Even armies themselves were not immune to the effects of imprecise precision bombing. In 1944, in Normandy, the Americans attempted an aerial bombardment prior to launching their big Operation *Cobra* attack. Unfortunately, the wind blew the smoke in the direction of the American lines and the bomber pilots, unable to see the ostensible target of a road for the smoke, bombed the smoke instead, killing many on their own side.

But military technology is not without its progressive qualities. Returning briefly to our engineer's approach to war, the more times a pilot is put over the target, the greater the chance that the aeroplane will be shot down and the pilot, trained at great expense, will be lost. If the bombs can be delivered accurately, the pilot only has to fly over the target once. Thus, in recent years the United States forces have given great attention to more accurate ways to hit the target. At first there were guided bombs, using lasers or radar. Now, microprocessor technology can be fitted to the bombs themselves, and global positioning co-ordinates can be entered by the pilot. The First Gulf War of 1991 was the first major display of such technologies and many pictures were shown of just how accurate the bombs were. Things have improved markedly since then. The result is that, as was seen in the 2003 Iraq campaign, a civilian has to be unlucky enough to live in the immediate vicinity of a likely target in order to become a 'collateral' victim of a bombing raid. Of course, since such air raids can also target things like water treatment plants or electrical generators, it is quite possible for the civilian to survive the bombing raid, only to perish as a consequence of more traditional non-combatant killers of wartime, such as disease.

Furthermore, these "wonder weapons" are only available to a few countries which are able to afford them. In many cases, the wars being waged in the world today are fought by armies which are not above the level of technology available to combatants in the Second World War. (Many conflicts, such as those occurring in West Africa, are below even this.) There is even a new type of warfare that expressly targets civilians, with terror campaigns often fought using suicide bombers who are willing to kill anyone who just happens to live in the wrong country or hold the wrong belief. The jet airliners turned into guided missiles on 11 September 2001 in the US cities of New York and Washington are the most notorious example, but there are plenty of civilians being killed or maimed elsewhere, such as in attacks on key targets in Israel like pizza parlours or buses. The front line in such conflicts is everywhere and nowhere at the same time.

Wars have become a staple of the daily news and there are many civilians who are in the business of providing the imagery that feeds the hunger of news organizations for such material. They have even made possible this book. Most war photographers are little known. Some, however, have become famous names, either for the quality of their images or for their historical role of being first. Roger Fenton, Felice Beato, Matthew Brady and his associates, Robert Capa, Bert Hardy, Cecil Beaton and James Nachtwey are all names whose work features in this book. Their work at times approaches the level of fine art, and some lesser known names have produced some of the most iconic images.

In addition to these news photographers, armies, navies and air forces also employ official photographers. Felice Beato is an example of one, employed by the British War Office. During the First World War and subsequent conflicts there have been many, including Frenchman Jean-Baptiste Tournassoud and Briton Geoffrey Malins. Official war photographers are now common in the military and naval forces of the most advanced countries. The US Department of Defense has employed a number to record events in Iraq. The work of such photographers provides the

ABOVE
Camouflaged US Marines patrol the Demilitarized Zone in the aftermath of the Tet offensive in Vietnam, 1968.

basis for great collections of war photographs, such as that found in the Imperial War Museum in London.

The pursuit of images of war has claimed a number of photographers' lives. Robert Capa survived the Spanish Civil War and the Second World War, only to perish when he stepped on a land mine while in search of new images with a French army patrol in Vietnam in 1954. Sean Flynn, who photographed British troops in Borneo during the "confrontation" with Indonesia, disappeared in Cambodia in 1970, having survived numerous trips "in country" in Vietnam with long-range reconnaissance patrols. Tim Page was luckier. He was wounded four times during his various excursions in Vietnam in the 1960s, and barely survived on the last occasion.

"War is Hell," warned American General William T. Sherman famously. The poorly educated Hooper, who would never have heard the statement, would probably still have had a taste for action even if he had. But let us conclude by thinking more of Charles Ryder and of his author, Evelyn Waugh. The episode I have quoted takes place aboard a train carrying Ryder back to a rendezvous with his pre-war past, one of fox-hunting parties, lavish meals and no shortages. Waugh wrote the book after his own personal encounter with war in Crete, where he no doubt felt the same desperate will to live as any soldier hunkering in a fox hole under mortar fire, or sailor trapped in a submarine being depth charged, or pilot flying a plane being riddled with shrapnel and bullets. *Brideshead Revisited* makes absolutely no allusion to such situations with good reason – one will rarely find a veteran willing to dwell upon them. Let all those who, like me, have been spared from such experiences, take a different attitude to Hooper. Let us pray that we are kept in ignorance.

Paul Brewer

THE FIRST IMAGES

Representations of warfare have a long history, stretching back to around 2500 BC, when carvings in Khufu's Great Pyramid and on the Stela of the Vultures depicted battle scenes. But for most of human history, such images were primarily works of art composed a considerable time after the events being depicted. Painting came to be the main method of showing war. The images were often artfully contrived to bring to prominence military leaders, or highlighting some key element in a battle. It was the development of photography in Europe in the first half of the nineteenth century which offered a new means of showing warfare.

However, it took some time for the technology of photographing people or objects to advance sufficiently to allow photographers to realize the immediacy possible with taking pictures. The first cameras were cumbersome things, while the chemical processes by which the pictures were captured did not help: it took a great deal of light, and a long exposure to take a decent photograph. Subjects had to remain stationary for a considerable length of time. Louis Daguerre's pioneering process required half an hour exposure, far too long for practical photography of human subjects. It was not until 1851, with the publication of the collodion process by Frederick Scott Archer, that exposure times were reduced to a more practical two or three seconds.

The collodion process required bulky equipment (glass plates measuring 10 x 12 inches), a lot of work, and a large quantity of water, but now it was possible for cameras to accompany armies in the field and navies across the ocean. The first major war to occur after Archer's invention was the Crimean War, which involved armies from France and Britain, two of the most technically advanced countries of the time. Both sent photographers to make pictures of the war, and soon after cameras were sent out specifically to record images of battles in India and China.

LEFT
A Roger Fenton photograph shows somewhat distracted British troops during the siege of Sevastapol.

THE CRIMEAN WAR 1854–1856

This conflict ostensibly originated in a dispute over the administration of the holy places in Jerusalem, then part of the Turkish Ottoman Empire. It was fought by a coalition of France, Britain, Ottoman Turkey and, later, the Kingdom of Sardinia against the Russian Empire. Russia's war against the Turks began in 1853, resulting in the occupation of Moldavia and Wallachia and the defeat of the Turkish fleet at the Black Sea port of Sinope by a Russian squadron which used guns firing shells, as opposed to the traditional naval weapons of round- and chain-shot. These early Russian successes resulted in intervention by France and Britain, who sent an army to lay siege to the port of Sevastopol in the Crimea, the main base of the Russian Black Sea. The Crimean port fell in September 1855. The war is mostly remembered for a mixture of military incompetence and disorganization that resulted in considerable hardship for the coalition soldiers. However, the conflict also featured the first use of armoured vessels in naval operations. They were included in the operations of the Franco-British fleets in the Baltic, a series of skilful campaigns now largely and unjustly forgotten, which drove the Russians to sue for peace.

ABOVE LEFT
Roger Fenton used this mobile dark room to develop the photographs he took during the Crimean War. He was one of three photographers (the others being James Robertson and the Frenchman Charles Langlois) who took pictures of the conflict, the first images of soldiers and scenes actually taken during a military conflict. However, the photographers avoided depicting the horrors of war – the dead and the wounded.

ABOVE
British soldiers photographed in camp. The uniforms would not look out of place on soldiers of the Napoleonic era (1800–1815). The collars have stiff, uncomfortable stocks to help hold the head erect. The red tunics and white crossbelts offer little in the way of camouflage, but since the smooth-bore muskets were only effective at a range of 50 yards, such considerations were insignificant.

ABOVE
British soldiers form up in camp in the Crimea. The formations adopted here, which are still used on the parade grounds of armies around the world, suited the military technology of the eighteenth century. The close order facilitated the effectiveness of comparatively inaccurate smoothbore muskets by concentrating the number of bullets into a small target area. This increased the probability of a hit. The price paid was to increase the number of potential targets on the firing side within a small area. Battles were won or lost on the results of such equations.

ABOVE
Cannonballs lie scattered on the battlefield of Balaclava. The battle owed its fame as much to the poetry of Tennyson as to the actual significance of the combat. The gallant charge of the British Light Brigade on Russian batteries in the North Valley passed into history as a symbol of British soldiers' courage and their leaders' incompetence. Yet the action was also marked by the timidity of Russian cavalry in attacking the 93rd Highlanders ("the Thin Red Line") and against the less memorable but more successful charge of the Heavy Brigade.

ABOVE
One of James Robertson's photographs shows some of the Russian fortifications of Sevastopol. The guns are on naval carriages, designed for easy handling in the cramped conditions of a ship's decks, and to be equally manoeuvrable within the narrow confines of an earthwork rampart. The siege set Russian skill in defence against the coalition's determination in attack. The Russian inability to conduct effective attacks against the coalition's siege works resulted in the port's capture.

RIGHT
One of Felice Beato's photographs taken at Lucknow shows the remains of dead mutineers scattered in the Secundra Bagh. Lucknow was besieged by the mutineers in July 1857. The garrison was reinforced in September, when a relieving force was unable to break the siege. A second relief force reached the city and stormed the Secundra Bagh on 16 November 1857, slaughtering its Indian defenders almost to a man.

THE INDIAN MUTINY 1857–1858

The Indian Mutiny was the last attempt by the "old" India of Hindu and Moslem princes to reverse the British takeover of the sub-continent. As British administrators challenged traditional Indian ways with modern, western ideas, the introduction into the Indian army of Enfield-rifled muskets, with separate measured powder cartridges, offered a pretext for rebellion. The fact that the cartridges were greased with cow and pig fat threatened the Hindu or Moslem native soldiers' religions, as each cartridge had to be bitten open during loading. Rebellion broke out at Meerut in May 1857. The rebels went from Meerut to occupy Delhi. Massacres of Europeans and Christians took place in both cities and elsewhere across the Ganges plain, but Bengal and its capital Calcutta remained loyal and offered British forces a base. It took just over a year to re-establish British rule over north-central and northwestern India. The war largely swept away old India, and laid foundations for a Western-style nationalism in India that eventually would triumph over British rule.

ABOVE
Another photograph by Felice Beato shows a British field piece in Delhi. Delhi was the initial focus for military operations, as the mutineers sought to utilize the prestige of Bahadur Shah, the last Mogul emperor, who was resident there. The British occupied the city after a ferocious street battle lasting about a week in September 1857. Beato was brother-in-law to James Robertson, and one or both was commissioned by the War Office to photograph scenes of the Mutiny.

THE SECOND OPIUM WAR 1856–1860

China's huge population presented many romantically minded nineteenth-century European and American businessmen with the hope of a vast market. However, their access to the country was severely restricted by the Chinese government. The First Opium War in 1839–1842 saw a Chinese attempt to restrict the importation of highly addictive opium militarily defeated by the British, and a treaty opening China to greater trade imposed. A further attempt by France and Britain in the late 1850s to increase trading privileges ultimately resulted in a second war. In August 1860, a military force seized the Taku forts at the mouth of the Peiho river, then advanced inland to occupy Beijing in October. The Chinese were forced to concede a further opening of their country to foreign trade – and also to allow Chinese labourers to emigrate for work elsewhere, a movement which eventually led to large Chinese communities in the United States and elsewhere.

ABOVE
Felice Beato also travelled to China to photograph scenes of the country and of the war. This picture shows the interior of one of the Taku forts after the assault of 21 August 1860. Dead Chinese, possibly moved by Beato and his assistants, lie in front of an embrasure, while scaling ladders used by French soldiers lean against the outside wall. As a symbol of Chinese technological inferiority, a crossbow sits atop the wooden embrasure.

THE AMERICAN CIVIL WAR

1861–1865

In 1861, the United States was among the most literate societies of its day, and its newspapers and magazines had large circulations. The Civil War generated a huge appetite for news, but, owing to technical limitations, none of these publications could reproduce photographs. Yet a large number of photographs related to the war were taken. Portrait photography became a fashionable, as soldiers had pictures taken of them to leave behind with their family or loved ones.

The simple fact that the war took place in an advanced, industrialized country with thousands of miles of railways was another factor in the increasing levels of photography during its course. There were an estimated 2,000 photographers at work in the country during the Civil War, and many of them saw an opportunity in taking pictures of scenes associated with the conflict.

The war itself was marked by many technological developments, many of them recorded photographically. Both armies were well equipped with rifled muskets. Breech-loading firearms with magazines carrying multiple rounds, such as revolvers and repeating rifles, were used for the first time on a wide scale, which had an impact on battle tactics. Many batteries on both sides were provided with shell-firing rifled artillery. Ships equipped with steam engines and armour were also deployed in substantial numbers.

The railway and the telegraph had a significant impact in keeping armies supplied, in moving troops on strategic operations and in communicating news rapidly to capitals, which allowed politicians – and the news media – more influence over military operations than ever. On many levels, the American Civil War foreshadowed developments in warfare that were to occur over the next hundred years.

LEFT
Intelligence officers of the Army of the Potomac taking time to relax outside their tent in 1864.

AMERICA AT WAR WITH HERSELF

In the 20 years preceding the American Civil War, slavery had been a cause of tension between the industrialized north-east states and the agrarian south, dividing communities and political parties. In the 1860 presidential election, Abraham Lincoln, a lawyer from Illinois, won by carrying almost all the northern states in an election contested by four candidates. His anti-slavery Republican party also gained a majority of seats in the House of Representatives and a plurality in the Senate. Faced with a government hostile to their way of life, the southernmost states seceded between December 1860 and February 1861. Lincoln called for the militia to enforce the laws in the seceded states, which had formed their own government – the Confederate States of America. When Confederate forces fired at Federal troops in Fort Sumter, a second group of southern states quit the Union. In the end, Lincoln committed the country to a war to preserve the Union and not to free slaves.

ABOVE

The Confederate "Stars and Bars" flies over captured Fort Sumter on 15 April 1861. The fort, in the middle of Charleston Harbor, became the trigger for war when the Confederates opened fire on the garrison and compelled the surrender of this Federal installation to the rebel government.

RIGHT

Men of the 1st Georgia Infantry regiment fought at the First Battle of Bull Run in July 1861. Like many militia units, both North and South, they wore blue uniforms. The confusion this could cause proved a decisive factor at Bull Run when the 33rd Virginia Infantry captured a key battery in the Federal line and turned the tide of the battle in the rebels' favour.

LEFT
A Federal corporal poses for the camera in full gear. The Federal armies were much better equipped than their rebel counterparts, in part owing to the greater industrialization of the northern economy, but also because of the effects of the blockade imposed by the Federal government on the rebel states.

ABOVE
A woman assists in a Federal army field kitchen. She was almost certainly married to one of the other soldiers working in the kitchen. Stews and soups were the easiest things to cook in such circumstances.

ABOVE
The pioneer photographer Matthew Brady stands (at right) with several of his assistants and the photographic equipment. Brady had been practising photography since 1843, but during the war he left the actual work in the hands of others, while he managed the business.

ABOVE
African-American soldiers stand on parade in camp in November 1864. From the outset of the war, there had been proposals to recruit African-Americans into the Federal Army. Formal organization and incorporation of African-American soldiers only came in May 1863, a few months after the Emancipation Proclamation was issued. They mostly served as labour battalions and garrison troops, although a few did see combat, including most famously the assault by the 54th Massachusetts Infantry on Fort Wagner in July 1863.

ABOVE
Supply wagons gather at Cumberland Landing during the 1862 Peninsula Campaign in eastern Virginia. Civil War armies were large, regularly numbering 75,000 to 100,000 soldiers. They required extensive logistical support to keep them armed and fed. The Federal army in particular demonstrated a capacity to supply its forces that was the equal of any of its professional European counterparts.

COMBAT

"Two armed mobs chasing each other round the country," was how Prussian general Count Helmuth von Moltke characterized the American Civil War. However, there was much to learn from the conflict for those who looked closely at the actual fighting. The war demonstrated the power of the rifled musket in defence, particularly in the spring and summer of 1864, when both main rebel armies dug in and forced the Federals to attack them. Casualties were heavy in these assaults, and in some ways they presaged the style of combat in the First World War. Rifled cannon were also deployed in large numbers, enabling targets a mile away to be engaged. Although their capabilities remained potential rather than actual, owing to technical limitations, these capabilities were demonstrated in combat for the first time. Finally, the longer ranges of rifled muskets compared to their smooth-bore antecedents, meant that infantry were for the first time able to deter cavalry charges through fire-power alone.

BELOW

Federal troops train during the winter of 1863–1864 in Chattanooga, Tennessee. They have adopted the classic assault formation of the war, with one or two companies of skirmishers advancing in front of the main body, which is drawn up in close order. The battle at this level was decided by a fire-fight between the ranks of both sides, until one or the other retired. However, as the war progressed, infantry adopted a different formation for attack, with some companies making short rushes forward, while others fired at the enemy.

OVERLEAF

General Ulysses S. Grant sits (left, with hat on knee) with the staff who had helped him defeat Rebel general Robert E. Lee in Virginia in April 1865. Grant was the greatest general the war produced. He recognized, as did Lincoln, that the way to defeat the Rebels was to destroy their armies in the field. His operational plan for the 1864 campaigns was a model of exerting pressure on the enemy across the whole combat zone. He also achieved significant successes as commander of the Union forces in the western theatre of the war, using his forces aggressively against both Rebel armies and their supply lines.

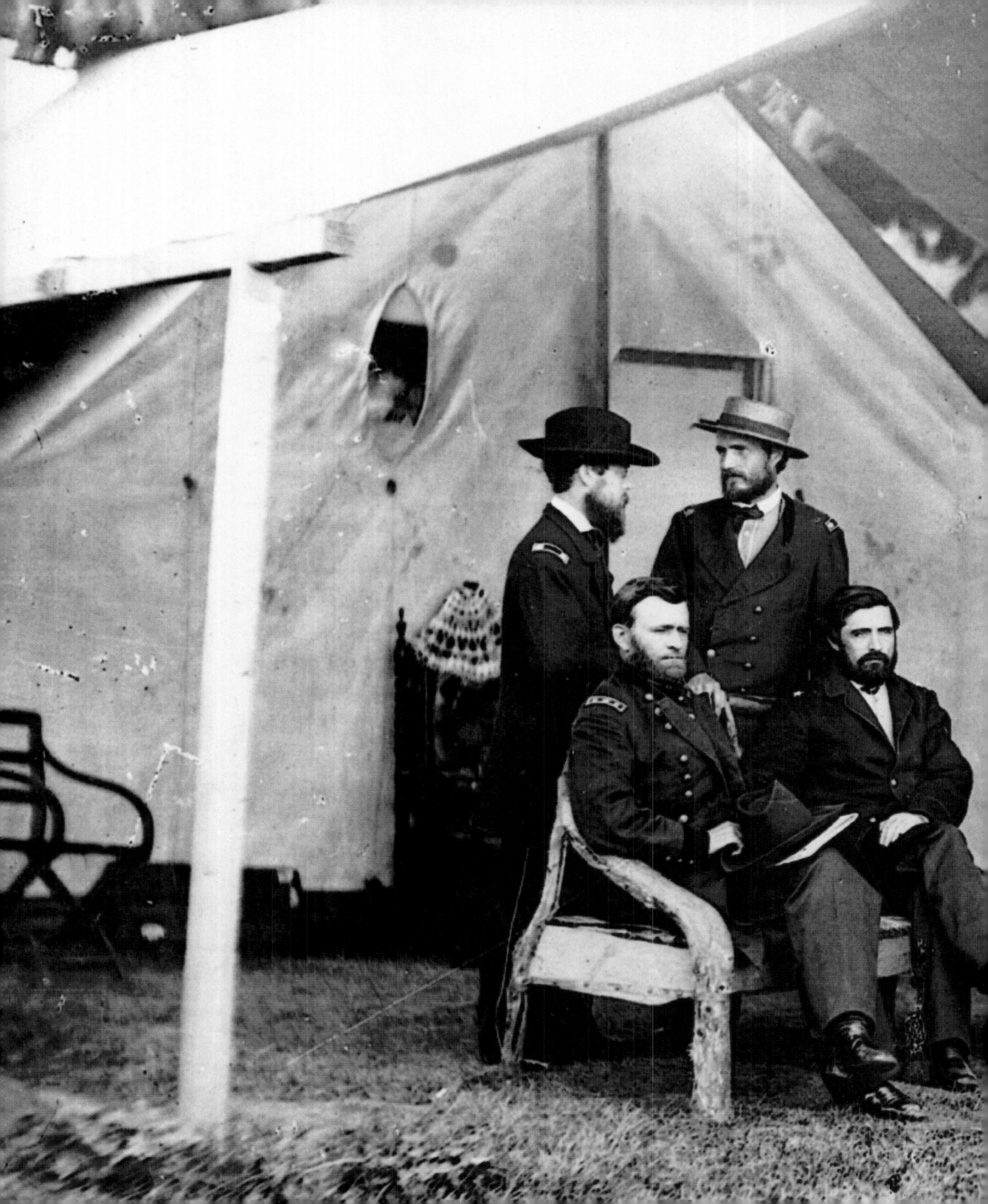

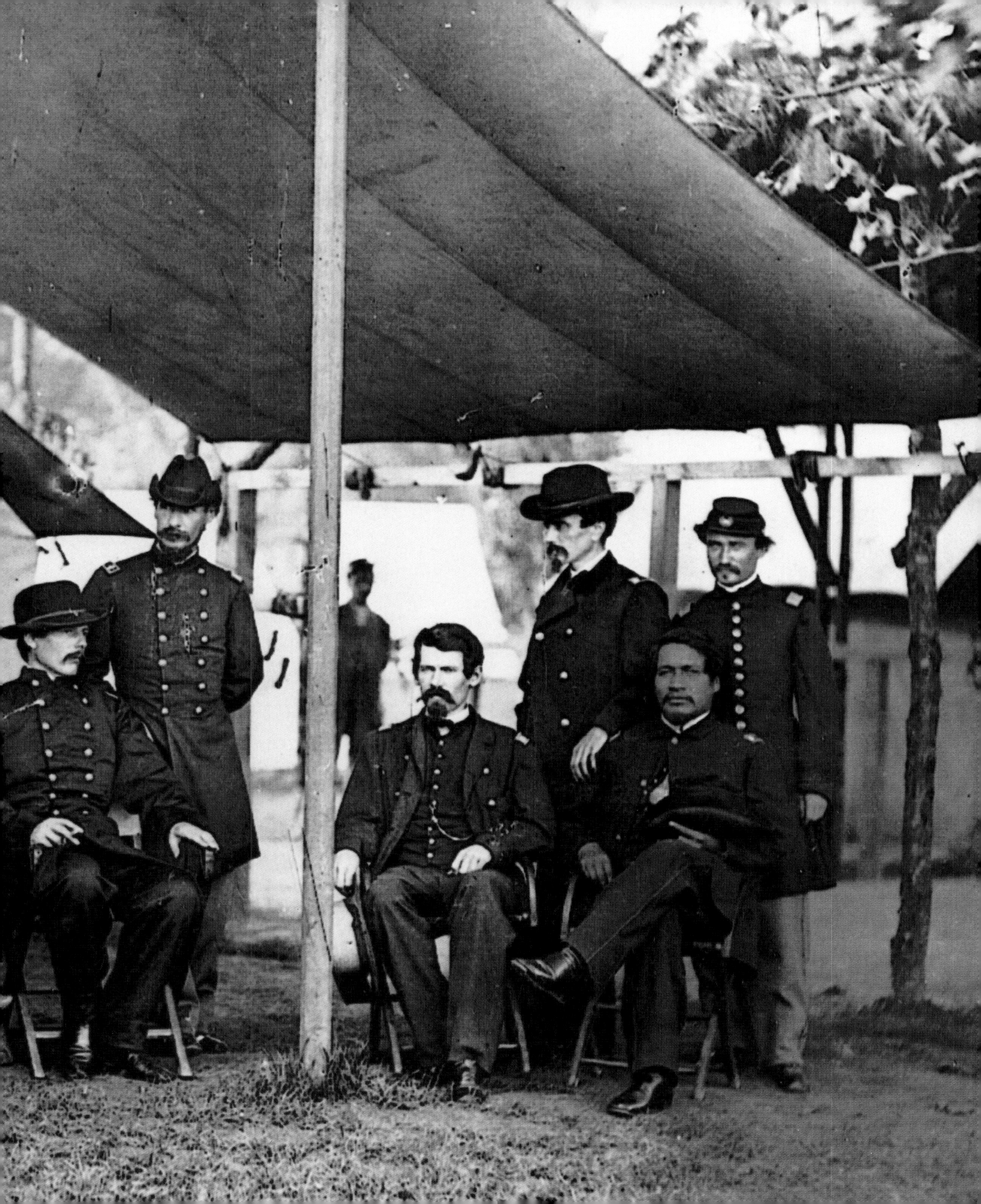

LEFT
Battery D of the 5th US Artillery deploys in a firing line, in a posed photograph taken by Timothy O'Sullivan. At the outset of the war, batteries such as this were attached to infantry brigades, but as the war progressed the value of massed fire became more evident to both sides, and regiments and even brigades of artillery were used. As with rifled muskets, this massed effect was more useful in defence than in attack.

THE WAR ON WATER

Although it held the larger portion of the 3,500-mile coastline of the United States in 1860, the Confederacy had no navy at the start of the war. This alone made the war at sea a one-sided affair. What it lacked in ships, the Confederacy made up for in the latest technology. It built a number of ironclad vessels, including the famous CSS *Virginia*. The *Virginia* took part in the first combat between ironclad vessels, when it battled the USS *Monitor* to a draw in March 1862. Other ironclads saw action in New Orleans, Charleston, and Mobile Bay, as well as along the Mississippi river and its tributaries. The war at sea was largely a routine matter where the Federal navy blockaded rebel ports, and occasionally supported amphibious landings to seize ports and forts. More dramatically, a number of key engagements were fought along the Mississippi as the Federal forces advanced along this important transportation artery to cut the Confederacy in two.

ABOVE

Sailors of the USS *Monitor* pass the time of day between watches in the summer of 1862. Unlike the CSS *Virginia*, which was effectively an armoured version of a broadside steamship, the *Monitor* utilized a turret that revolved to bring the guns to bear. A dent caused by enemy fire appears on the turret. The *Monitor* sank in a storm off Cape Hatteras in December 1862.

ABOVE
The USS *Cairo* gets up steam while moored on a river. The ironclads of the seacoast had their counterparts on the rivers, which pre-dated the construction of the *Monitor*. River gunboats like the *Cairo* provided effective support to the army's operations against Forts Donelson and Henry in 1862, and against Vicksburg in 1863.

OVERLEAF
The crew of a Federal gunboat pose for the camera, including a number of African-Americans. The Federal navy recruited African-Americans from the outset of the war, but for the most part they experienced the dull routine of blockading the rebel coastline. For the majority of these men, the only excitement of the war (apart from rough weather) was if their ship gave chase to a rebel blockade-runner, an event that also brought the possible bonus of prize money.

ABOVE
Professor Thaddeus Lowe's balloon is inflated for an ascent to observe rebel lines in the spring of 1862. Lowe had been promoting the uses of his balloon at the outset of the war. The Federal commander of the attack on the Rebel capital Richmond, Virginia, General George B. McClellan, enthusiastically hired Lowe to give him a high vantage point to see the enemy deployments. This was the first systematic use of aerial observation in war.

INNOVATIONS

The American Civil War was marked by a number of innovations in warfare. This arose in part from the dynamism of mid-nineteenth-century science and technology. It also owed something to the highly politicized nature of American society: someone well-connected politically was always willing to support a programme that could receive some kind of funding from the government. Thanks to the far greater quantity of factories and engineers it possessed, the North was better able to put some of these ideas into production. The armies of both sides made considerable use of railways, and this development had by far the single largest impact on the war. Whereas before, an army of 30,000 men was about the limit of what could be supplied by wagon and forage, now railways could feed and maintain a 100,000-strong army for offensive operations along a single axis of advance. But beyond this dramatic shift, there were also smaller innovations which foreshadowed technical developments in warfare over the next 50 years.

ABOVE
Rebel soldiers built these log breastworks and rifle pits for the battle at Spotsylvania Court House in May 1864. Although such fieldworks were in themselves nothing new, the armies of both sides were more enthusiastic about "digging in" than had been the case in previous wars. Even battles in which manoeuvre played an important role, such as Antietam in September 1862 and Gettysburg in July 1863, were characterized by improvised defensive works using stone walls and sunken roads.

LEFT
These *chevaux de frise* were another form of field engineering that had been inherited from previous wars but saw extensive deployment during the Civil War. They were basically a chain of pointed stakes that were placed in the way of any likely direction of advance by the enemy. They were more portable than stakes simply stuck in the ground, and could be moved more easily to open a gap in a defensive fieldwork to launch a counter-attack.

BELOW
A waterlogged rebel trench at Petersburg, Virginia, in April 1865 would not have looked out of place in Flanders in 1917. Full-scale trench systems were used around Atlanta in 1864, and during the siege of Petersburg (June 1864 to April 1865), foreshadowing the First World War's deadlock on the Western Front.

RIGHT
A Federal cavalryman poses with his seven-shot repeating Spencer carbine. By the end of the war, the Federal army deployed several units armed with repeating breech-loaders, and while these did not in themselves prove battle-winners, they did give the Federal forces yet another important advantage over their opponents.

U.S.

LEFT

Telegraphists of the Federal army take a break. The military use of the telegraph was another of the war's important innovations. Mobile telegraph wagons such as this could be connected to an already-existing telegraph line and communications could then be established with the President and General-in-Chief in Washington, D.C. Telegraph wires were key targets of raiding parties on both sides, and the rapid flow of information enabled reinforcements to be rushed to threatened areas as quickly as railway transport would allow.

IMPERIAL ADVENTURES

1860–1914

At the end of the fifteenth century, the states of Europe began to expand their influence far beyond their home continent. Trading posts established abroad by Europeans often began life as fortresses, and these permanent military presences gradually developed into direct political control. In the nineteenth century, a system of colonial empires reached its full blossoming. After 1860, wars between the natives of the colonized regions of Africa and Asia and the European imperialist powers displayed the vast technological gulf between them.

The development of breech-loading weapons and magazine rifles increased the lethality and rate of fire available to armies. Whereas a muzzle-loading rifled musket might achieve a rate of fire of two or three rounds a minute at an effective range of 200 yards (183 metres), the magazine rifle could easily achieve double that rate at longer ranges of 500 to 900 yards (457 to 823 metres). The tactical advantage that less-advanced societies had often once possessed through their superiority in numbers now vanished. Add a comparable revolution in artillery to this "small-arms revolution", and the European technological advantage on the battlefield became a decisive one.

Photography accompanied these wars abroad. Increasingly sophisticated chemical processes and the portability of cameras and development equipment enabled the photographer's art to advance far beyond the graphic artist's sketch-book or paints in capturing an exact moment. Artful arrangement of a scene became less common, and photographs more and more showed events as they really happened.

LEFT
Officers of the 1st regiment of the French Foreign Legion in Algiers, c. 1900.

THE ANGLO-ZULU WAR, 1879

The war grew out of a border dispute between the Zulu nation and Boers (settlers of Dutch descent) in South Africa. In 1877, Britain annexed the Transvaal, previously an independent Boer republic, bringing the British empire into the dispute. The British attempted to impose controls on the Zulu army, which were rejected, and in 1879 an invasion of Zululand was launched. The Zulu army was disciplined and well trained. The Zulus were also tactically astute, and their battle formation was a model of the basic military principles of using manoeuvre and mass to defeat the enemy. The British, however, were technically far superior, as well as being equally disciplined and highly motivated. The initial Zulu victory at Isandhlwana in January 1879 was not followed up effectively, and heavy casualties caused by European firearms affected the efficiency of the Zulu army. Another invasion of Zululand was launched in March and by July the Zulu nation had been conquered.

ABOVE

Members of the Natal Native Contingent, armed with muzzle-loading rifles, sit during a break in the campaign. The British employed thousands of African auxiliary troops in the war, who were normally enrolled in the Natal Native Contingent. They were issued uniforms and weapons and subject to a degree of European-style discipline.

ABOVE
A Zulu chieftain sits astride a mule while meeting with John Dunn (right). Dunn was an Englishman who lived among the Zulus, virtually as one of them, both before and after the war.

BELOW

Survivors of the British defence of the mission station at Rorke's Drift sit for a photograph after the battle. This astonishing affair, the subject of the famous film *Zulu*, pitted 139 British soldiers against several thousand Zulu warriors. Eleven Victoria Crosses, Britain's highest award for gallantry in battle, were won by the defenders, the highest total for any single engagement in British military history.

ABOVE

Ruined buildings of Alexandria after the bombardment of 11 July 1882. It was one of the largest British naval operations since the end of the Crimean War, as a fleet of eight battleships and 11 gunboats engaged the shore defences of the Egyptian city. After five hours of shelling, the Egyptians abandoned the defences and, later that day, the city.

ARABI'S REVOLT 1882

European influence in Egypt following the construction of the Suez Canal, and a growing financial crisis, provoked a mutiny in 1881 by some army officers, led by Colonel Ahmed Arabi. The uprising resulted in some reforms to the constitution of the country's government. In 1882, France and Britain, the countries that had financed the construction of the canal, demanded in turn that Arabi's reforms be checked. The Egyptian government collapsed, and Arabi became the dominant politician in the country. Anti-European rioting broke out in Alexandria in June 1882, and in response a British fleet, stationed offshore to observe the crisis, bombarded the city and landed troops to "restore order". This act fanned Anti-European sentiment, and a revolt spread throughout Egypt. The British then sent an army, which in September 1882 defeated the Egyptian forces at the Battle of Tel el-Kebir. Britain then took control of Egypt, established an important naval base at Alexandria, and remained as the country's effective ruler until 1952.

ABOVE
A photographer's assistant points to the barrel of an Egyptian gun that experienced a direct hit during the shelling. The bombardment was perhaps the archetypal incident of "gunboat diplomacy", being an exclusively naval intervention to secure an immediate restoration of the preceding status quo.

THE MAXIM MACHINE GUN

The machine gun was, more than the magazine rifle, the epitome of the mechanization of firepower. Gatling guns, Gardner guns and mitrailleuses preceded the Maxim gun as attempts to harness some level of mechanization to shooting. But each of these required the intervention of a human operator to control a recoil mechanism. The Maxim gun, however, allowed push-button shooting – after pressing the trigger, the recoil of the firing mechanism itself cleared the breech and loaded the next round. The result was a tremendous rate of fire for the time, practically 300 rounds per minute.

BELOW
Sir Hiram Maxim, the Maxim machine gun's inventor, sits at a wheeled carriage equipped with one of his inventions. Maxim was an American who settled in Britain. After his invention of the machine gun, he became fascinated with heavier-than-air flight, although none of his concepts got off the ground.

FRANCE'S COLONIAL EMPIRE

The French colonial empire covered much of north-western Africa, parts of central Africa and Indochina, plus remnants of an earlier empire in the Americas. Algeria was already under French control at the time of the Crimean War, while Napoleon III established a French presence in Indochina, but most of the empire was acquired after the Franco-Prussian War of 1870–1871. Sustained military activity took place in Indochina, starting with the seizure of Hanoi in 1882, and a campaign against the "Black Flag Pirates". The Chinese resisted the French invasion, and a brief war included the short naval battle at Foochow, where a French squadron destroyed the Chinese navy's most modern ships. The French then gradually expanded throughout the rest of Indochina. In West Africa, French wars against Dahomey in 1892 and the Mandingo during the 1880s and 1890s established French authority there. By the end of the nineteenth century, the French had secured an empire second only to the British.

ABOVE
Officers of the 1st Regiment of the French Foreign Legion sit for a photograph, c.1900. The Foreign Legion's romantic reputation was in part a construct of Hollywood films, but it established a formidable reputation as a fighting force during the French intervention in Mexico in 1861–1867; in North Africa throughout the nineteenth century; and in Indochina in the 1880s.

AN AMERICAN EMPIRE

The United States fought a major war against Mexico in 1845–1847, and several minor ones against Native Americans in the West throughout the nineteenth century. US forces took control of a vast hinterland that stretched from the Mississippi to the Pacific Ocean. The Plains Wars and wars in the South-west swept away a whole people in order to create suitable conditions for the industrial exploitation of the Great Plains, the Great Basin and to unite the Pacific coastal states with the East by means of railways. With the "closing" of the frontier in 1890, the United States increasingly looked to exploiting markets abroad, and using military force to secure an American presence. In 1898, a war with Spain brought the Philippines, Puerto Rico and Guam under American control, and the former became the setting for a fierce war with various Filipino groups, which opposed exchanging one colonial master for another.

BELOW
The body of Big Foot, chief of the Sioux at Pine Ridge reservation, lies frozen in the snow at Wounded Knee, South Dakota, after the massacre of 29 December 1890. The Sioux (or Lakota, as they are properly known) fought several wars in a vain attempt to preserve their way of life. These wars have acquired a legendary status in American military history, but were frequently punctuated with ugly massacres, perpetrated by both sides.

ABOVE

American troops stand with their Gatling gun during the occupation of the Philippines. The Americans were ceded the Philippines after their victory over Spain in 1898. There were already rebels fighting their Spanish overlords, and these had expected the Americans to grant rights of self-government to the Filipinos. The Philippine-American War lasted from 1899 until 1902, although fighting against the Moros, Muslims on the island of Mindanao, lasted until 1913.

THE BOER WAR 1899–1902

The British annexation of the Boer republic in the Transvaal was reversed in 1881 when, after a short war, the Boers regained their independence. However, the discovery of gold in the Witwatersrand created tension over foreign residents' rights, and war broke out again between Britain and the Boers of Transvaal and the Orange Free State. The Boers at first achieved significant successes, including "Black Week" in December 1899 when the British were badly beaten in three separate engagements. A reinforced British army succeeded in occupying the Boer republics by June 1900, and a two-year guerrilla war followed until the Boers finally surrendered. The war was marked by a clear illustration of the fire-power potential of magazine rifles used by skilled marksmen occupying strong defensive positions against old-fashioned mass attacks. The British also employed "concentration camps", Boer civilians were placed to reduce the ability of the guerrillas to move freely and receive supplies from a friendly population.

ABOVE
British soldiers take aim from a trench position. The British initially approached battles with the Boers in the same manner as they had tackled any number of other opponents in colonial warfare. They advanced in column, then deployed in line to deliver volleys of fire on the enemy position. Consequently, the British suffered heavy casualties, as their deployment zone was within the range of the Boers' Mauser rifles.

LEFT
A Naval Brigade gun fires on Boer positions. Initially, British artillery was relatively ineffective, and outranged by the Boers' guns throughout the war. As the conflict progressed, the army became more effective at co-ordinating its shooting, especially useful in covering the withdrawal of shattered British attacks. Direct fire against enemy targets was perceived as less useful than indirect mass barrages, although the British did not completely incorporate this into their military doctrine after the war.

ABOVE
Boer troops defend a dug-in position. The Boers emphasized defensive tactics in battle, finding positions that enabled a flattish firing trajectory for their rifles, typically the forward slope of a hill or ridge rather than its crest.

ABOVE
A British balloon during the march on Johannesburg in 1901. The British made considerable use of balloons during the campaign, a system of observation suited to the rolling terrain of the veldt, although hardly a secretive one.

THE BOXER REBELLION

The "Fists of Righteous Harmony", better known in English as the Boxers, was an anti-Western Chinese nationalist movement that emerged in 1898, which launched an uprising against Western influence in the empire in 1899. In June 1899, the Boxers moved from attacking Chinese Christians and Western missionaries to a direct attack on the foreign legations in Tientsin and Peking in association with the Imperial Chinese army. The siege of the legations started on 20 June and lasted 55 days, until a relief expedition arrived from the coast. Initially, the force on the coast believed the legations had been massacred and did not hurry to relieve them. Another, much shorter siege occurred at Tientsin. The alliance of Western nations, plus Japan, assembled a large army at Tientsin and on 4 August began the advance on Peking, relieving the legations on 14 August. The Chinese government, which had formally declared war on the foreign powers, agreed a peace treaty on 7 September 1901, after a campaign of terror and atrocity by the foreign armies in pursuit of the Boxers.

RIGHT

This drawing, based on a photograph, shows the execution of Boxers by Chinese authorities. The use by the Chinese government of judicial procedures against its own people at the behest of the foreign powers underlined its powerlessness. After the Boxer Rebellion, the Chinese imperial regime was totally discredited. Republican movements that agitated for the ending the Unequal Treaties – which denied the Chinese authority over Europeans in their country – gathered influence.

ABOVE
British, French, American, Russian, Japanese, Austro-Hungarian, German, and Italian soldiers assemble for a portrait at Peking. The Boxer Rebellion was suppressed by this eight-nation alliance, and represented a rare instance of great powers allying against a single foe.

ABOVE
A view of an encampment outside Tientsin, the city that served as the main base of operations against the Boxers. The eight powers assembled a 20,000-strong army to relieve the siege at Peking, and further reinforcements led to around 100,000 foreign troops being deployed in the suppression of the Boxer Rebellion.

WARS BETWEEN THE GREAT POWERS

1860–1914

Europe was the scene of several important wars between 1860 and the outbreak of the First World War. The most important were the Wars of German Unification, which included the Schleswig–Holstein War of 1864, the Austro–Prussian War of 1866, and the Franco–Prussian War of 1870–1871. These conflicts transformed the European political landscape by creating a new German Empire that threatened the balance of power on the continent. The Prussian army that triumphed in each of these campaigns was perhaps the most efficient military service in history. Unlike all the other military forces of the Great Powers, it turned the art of war into a science, and its soldiers trained and studied for combat with the dedication of sportsmen. The Prussian army set a standard that all other armies attempted to attain, and which few could manage.

This era was also marked by wars that heralded the arrival of new powers outside Europe. The United States had long been considered a potentially powerful nation, but one which was more interested in its own economic development than foreign conquests. This changed in 1898, with a war against Spain that ended in American victory. More significant was the Russo–Japanese War of 1904–1905, in which the Russian empire was defeated on land and sea. In another landmark shift in world politics, the peace deal was mediated by the United States.

Technologically, this era was a transitional one, as the effectiveness of rapid fire weapons and better explosives continued the shift in favour of defence. This was countered by more and more dispersed formations moving forwards by rushes rather than advances in column.

LEFT
A barricade in Paris during the Communard uprising of 1871.

ABOVE
A regimental band of the Prussian army. The Prussian army was successful in the field, but suffered heavy casualties in attacks on fortresses. Their study of this problem laid the foundations for their victories in 1866 and 1870–1871.

THE SCHLESWIG–HOLSTEIN WAR OF 1864

This small-scale war stemmed from a border dispute between the Kingdom of Denmark and the German Confederation. The Danes sought to annex the Duchy of Schleswig, which had a substantial population of German speakers. The Prussians objected strongly and, with Austrian support, invaded. The war began in April 1864, and was rapidly marked by the defeat of the Danes at Dybbøl, and the occupation of Jutland. Meanwhile, in May the Danes defeated an Austrian squadron at the battle of Helgoland. The Prussians scored a major victory in June on the island of Als. A truce was agreed at the end of October, and in November a peace treaty allowed for Schleswig to pass into Prussian control, while Austria took over the administration of the Duchy of Holstein to the south.

ABOVE
A mobile farrier unit works during the war. Nineteenth-century armies relied heavily on cavalry for scouting and horse-drawn vehicles for supplies. An army's farriers played the same important role that mechanics of the Second World War did in keeping the army's transport in running order.

THE AUSTRO–PRUSSIAN WAR, 1866

The Austrian Habsburg Empire was a collection of nationalities, including Germans, which were ruled by the family that had supplied Holy Roman Emperors from the Middle Ages until Napoleon's termination of the institution in 1806. However, just as the emperors had been the traditional overlords of Germany, they still performed a vestigial part of this role in the German Confederation that was created after the Napoleonic Wars ended in 1815. Disputes between Prussia and Austria over the administration of Schleswig and Holstein following the end of the 1864 war resulted in Austria declaring war on Prussia. Most German states supported Austria; Prussia had support from Italy, which itself had emerged victorious from a war with Austria in 1859. The Prussians rapidly invaded Bohemia, and through effective infantry tactics and astute strategic manoeuvres crushed the Austrian army at the Battle of Königgrätz on 3 July 1866. The Italians, meanwhile, were defeated in a naval battle at Lissa on 20 July. Austria sued for peace, and Prussia took control of a new North German Confederation, while Italy gained the Veneto.

THE FRANCO–PRUSSIAN WAR 1870–1871

Prussia's victory over Austria left France as its only rival for the claim to be the leading power in Europe. The Prussian chancellor, Otto von Bismarck, who had masterminded Prussia's burgeoning political role since 1862, formulated a diplomatic trap over the Spanish monarchy that the French emperor, Napoleon III, blundered into. War broke out, and the Prussian army defeated the main French forces in a matter of weeks. However, France, unlike Austria, did not give up so easily. Napoleon III had been captured, but an ad hoc republican government continued the resistance. The war dragged on through the winter of 1870, with Paris undergoing a desperate siege while French armies attempted to relieve it. With the capital virtually starved into submission, the French sued for peace. Prussia proclaimed a German empire and annexed the French territories of Alsace and Lorraine. A coda to the war came with the proclamation of a workers' Commune (which effectively meant an independent government) in Paris shortly after the peace treaty was signed in February 1871. The bloody suppression of the Commune passed into radical political legend.

LEFT

A battery of Prussian artillery poses for a group photograph. Although the Prussian army's Dreyse rifle was heavily outclassed by the French Chassepot, the Prussian artillery was deployed more effectively and had better range and explosives, which resulted in their victory over the French.

OVERLEAF

One of the earliest photographs purporting to show a battle in progress, captures a moment during the battle of Sedan, 2 September 1870. Infantry are advancing in columns on the right, while another unit is deployed in skirmish order across the field on the left. The battle was a victory for the Prussians, who manouevred the French into a trap and surrounded them, forcing an entire army to surrender. It was the model for subsequent German military operations in two world wars.

ABOVE
A balloon is inflated in the Place St Pierre, Paris. The Parisians made extensive use of balloons to transmit messages to the armies attempting to break the siege of the city. The balloons had to be made in Paris, since it was difficult to fly them back. Leon Gambetta, the minister of the interior, made use of a balloon to fly out of Paris to Tours in October 1870 to help organize the war effort.

THE SPANISH–AMERICAN WAR 1898

A Cuban uprising against the Spanish in the 1890s reawakened a long-standing American interest in the island. As the war dragged on over several years and allegations were made of Spanish atrocities, American sympathy for the Cubans mounted. In January 1898 the American government sent the USS *Maine* to Havana to protect Americans considered to be threatened by the war. On 15 February 1898 the *Maine* exploded and sank. War fever over allegations that the ship was destroyed by a Spanish mine led to an American expedition being authorized to end the civil war and free Cuba. Spain declared war. The war was short. In May, an American squadron sank a Spanish one in Manila in the Philippines. In June, the Americans began landing troops in Cuba. In July, the Spanish Atlantic Fleet was sunk trying to escape from Santiago de Cuba, and American land forces captured Santiago itself. The United States occupied Puerto Rico, and in August hostilities ended.

BELOW

The wreck of the USS *Maine* rests in Manila harbour. At the time, the theory that she was destroyed by a mine was widely accepted. A 1911 US Navy department enquiry examined the wreck and agreed with the mine theory, but a 1976 book by a US Navy admiral, using extensive scientific analysis, took the view that the destruction was caused by spontaneous combustion in a coal bunker that was situated on the other side of a bulkhead to a magazine.

ABOVE
Soldiers of the 16th Infantry, US Army, crouch in the hollow of San Juan Creek, during the battle of San Juan Hill, 1 July 1898. The battle was the biggest land engagement of the war, and was marked by Spanish rifles taking a heavy toll on the attacking Americans, until the Spanish position was enfiladed by Gatling gun fire from nearby Kettle Hill.

RIGHT
Lieutenant-Colonel Theodore Roosevelt stands with members of the 1st US Volunteer Cavalry, the famous "Rough Riders". The regiment was formed of volunteers from the south-western United States, and Roosevelt's prominent role in its actions during the Cuban campaign helped secure him nomination as the vice-presidential candidate of the Republican party in the 1900 presidential election.

THE RUSSO-JAPANESE WAR

The Japanese had defeated the Chinese in the Sino-Japanese War of 1894–1895, a conflict provoked by Chinese objections to Japanese support for reformists in Korea. Japan acquired Port Arthur as part of the spoils of victory, but Russia, which had its own ambitions for Manchuria and Korea, compelled the Japanese to surrender it back to China. The Russians then negotiated their own lease of a naval base at Port Arthur, and also sent troops into Manchuria. Japan waited six years, and then, in 1904, launched a surprise attack against Port Arthur and into Manchuria. The war revolved around control of the seas between Japan and China and control of the railway through Manchuria. After a siege of Port Arthur that ended in the naval base's capture, fierce fighting in Manchuria and two heavy naval defeats, the Russians were forced to negotiate peace, mediated by President Theodore Roosevelt of the United States.

ABOVE
Japanese soldiers rest on the heights overlooking Port Arthur. The siege pitted Japanese infantry assaults against Russian troops who employed barbed wire and machine guns, almost a rehearsal for the trench warfare of the First World War. This war saw the first use of modern-style hand grenades.

ABOVE
The Russian battleship *Tsesarevitch* interned at Tsingtao after the Battle of the Yellow Sea in August 1904. The Russian Pacific Squadron was trapped in Port Arthur by the Japanese fleet, but as the Japanese siege tightened around the city, the Russian garrison commander thought it wiser to break out. The Japanese fleet caught the Russian squadron and defeated it in a running battle, thanks to a hit on the *Tsesarevitch* that damaged her steering.

ABOVE
Russian ships, destroyed by shelling from Japanese land artillery, lie aground in Port Arthur harbour. Port Arthur fell in January 1905. The Russians sent their Baltic Fleet around Africa, but the force was destroyed at the battle of Tsushima in May 1905.

RIGHT
Japanese infantry rest in camp. As well as their naval victories, the Japanese also defeated the Russian field army at Mukden in March 1905. The battles in Manchuria saw superior Japanese tactics overcome stout Russian defences, albeit at the cost of heavy casualties. The Russian defeat led to a revolution in European Russia and the loss of its influence in China.

THE BALKAN WARS 1912–1913

In 1912, European Turkey, still encompassed much of the modern Balkans. However, several small states had gained independence from Turkey during the nineteenth century, including Romania, Serbia, Montenegro and Greece. Bulgaria joined them in the early years of the twentieth century. In 1912, with the tacit support of Russia, these countries attacked Turkey. The resulting First Balkan War lasted from 8 October until 30 May 1913, and the Balkan states almost swept the Turks out of Europe. However, Bulgaria, did rather too well out of the peace settlement for the taste of its allies, while Greece was unhappy at Austro-Hungarian and Italian pressure to create an independent Albania out of land it had expected to receive. In June 1913, in order to forestall an expected assault, the Bulgarians themselves attacked Serbian and Greek forces in Macedonia. The former allies of Bulgaria, joined by Turkey, now waged a brief war that lasted until 10 August 1913. The whole affair was a war by proxy among the Great Powers, with Germany and Austria-Hungary sympathetic to Turkey and subsequently Bulgaria, while Russia supported the rest.

LEFT

Balkan irregulars take up firing positions for the camera. Although the main European powers had a somewhat patronizing view of the conflict, of little mini-states aping their betters, the Balkan Wars were largely fought by well-trained armies, armed with modern equipment.

LEFT
A Bulgarian battery dug in for an indirect fire role during the Second Balkan War. One of the great discoveries of observers of the Boer War and, more especially, the Russo-Japanese War, was the value of indirect artillery fire. Previously, artillery engaged targets it could see, following the infantry closely, and attempting to achieve destructive effects with rapid fire. Now, it became more important to identify targets (such as concentrations of enemy troops or artillery) and transmit this information to the artillery, allowing it to remain concealed yet still achieve destructive effects.

THE FIRST WORLD WAR

1914–1918

"The war to end war", the skilfully crafted phrase of British novelist H. G. Wells, made into a slogan by US President Woodrow Wilson, has always been associated with the First World War. Yet Wells coined the phrase in 1914, before the full scale of the horror had yet been visited upon the armies of Europe.

The stalemate in the trenches was a product of new war technologies. The machine gun, telephone lines, quick-firing recoil mechanisms and high-explosive shells all contributed to the deadlock. Both sides sought some technological way out. The Germans deployed poison gas in the spring of 1915. The British rolled out the tank in 1916. However, mobile warfare was only restored through the more imaginative use of weapons that had been available in 1914. The Germans discovered that speed and concentration of forces were the secrets, lessons that have been applied to every subsequent war.

The war shattered the old political system, as four empires were swept away and a national home in Palestine was promised to the Jews, a source of future conflict. Fighting also took place in the imperial possessions around the globe: the Far East, German East Africa and Southwest Africa and the war even visited the remote Falkland Islands.

This was also the first war where the press played a significant role. For the first time, those not directly involved in the conflict could not ignore the images of war. The new illustrated newspapers relied on photographs for their eye-catching content. Films were commissioned by governments to encourage the war effort, and the invention of film processing and small, portable cameras allowed the photographer's eye to be more intrusive than ever before.

LEFT
British medics dole out a rum ration to wounded German prisoners.

THE WAR BEGINS

Debates about the inevitability of and responsibility for the First World War still trouble historians, with the conflict seeming in hindsight unnecessary and avoidable. Yet without doubt the Great Powers of Europe seemed determined on some kind of reckoning that would resolve whether Germany would be the greatest among them. In 1914 even though every national and military leader knew the conflict would be difficult and costly, Europe went to war. The alliance system brought on the war with the inexorability of an avalanche. Then, the Germans attacked through Belgium, and the British went to war against the Germans.

ABOVE
On 28 June 1914, during a visit to Sarajevo, the heir to the Austro-Hungarian throne, Archduke Franz Ferdinand, was shot by a Serbian nationalist, Gavrilo Princip. Here, the archduke descends the steps of the town hall to the waiting limousine. Had the driver not taken a wrong turn, Princip might not have had his opportunity to fire the fatal shots.

ABOVE
Across Europe crowds celebrated the coming of war, the time of reckoning that had long been awaited. This crowd in Munich included a young Adolf Hitler (indicated in the circle), who would join a regiment of the Bavarian army and experience front-line combat first hand.

LEFT
The French 21st Infantry Regiment parades through Rouen in August 1914. The French went to war in largely the same uniforms they had worn in 1870, with dark blue greatcoats and bright red trousers. The red was easy to see at a distance and French casualties in the attack were consequently high. The colourful uniforms of the past were no longer practical in a world of long-range fire-power.

THE OPENING CAMPAIGNS

All the countries that went to war had drawn up careful plans for fighting it. In the East, the Russians struck at Germany through Prussia and at Austria through Galicia. In the West, the French attacked into Alsace and Lorraine, the provinces lost after the 1870 war with Germany. The Germans, however, sought to outflank the main French armies with an offensive through Belgium, where they would encounter British forces arrayed to defend the territorial integrity of the Low Countries. During August 1914, the German plans succeeded, as their holding forces in Alsace and Lorraine halted the French attacks and sheer weight of numbers forced the Belgian and British armies to retreat. French attempts to react to the German plan failed until, in September 1914, a week-long battle along the Marne enabled the French, with British support, to take advantage of the overstretched German armies and push them back. Meanwhile, in the East, the outnumbered Germans destroyed a Russian army in the Tannenberg campaign, while the Russians succeeded in their attack on Galicia until their overextended supply lines forced a halt.

ABOVE
A still from a film taken by British cameraman, J. Frank Brockliss, shows Belgian troops defending a hastily thrown together road-block in the town of Alost. The film showed the Belgian troops under fire and then rushing forward to attack, before retiring. Shortly after Brockliss left, they abandoned the position.

ABOVE
The first months of the war saw desperate measures taken to move troops to the front. Most famously, 1,200 Parisian taxicabs were used by General Gallieni to move part of his garrison to the front. Here, in October 1914, London omnibuses serve in the transport fleet of the British Expeditionary Force.

ABOVE
All countries understood that airplanes and airships added a new dimension to warfare. However, they were initially used largely as reconnaissance craft, or to drop a few hand grenades to harass a concentration of troops. Air-to-air fighting was so far restricted to taking pot shots with rifles from the cockpit. A sentry stands watch over British aircraft.

THE STALEMATE IN THE TRENCHES

After the battle of the Marne, the Germans withdrew to the heights around the Aisne river. This proved an excellent position and they decided instead to try and outflank the Allies. The battle of Ypres followed and both sides discovered that machine guns were very effective in defence, if dug in as part of a network of trenches. And so a long strip of field fortifications snaked its way across France and Belgium, from the North Sea to the Swiss border, resulting in no more mobile warfare in the West for nearly four years.

ABOVE
German and British soldiers fraternize during the Christmas Truce of 1914. This unofficial cease-fire has entered into the mythology of pacifism, but at the time it was not seen as anything more than a moment when the celebration of the season of goodwill was shared by honoured foes.

RIGHT
A German soldier attempts to ward off trench-foot in a Flanders trench in 1914. The condition could cause the loss of toes, and it was important to keep the feet dry to avoid it. Changing socks frequently was recommended. The wet and miserable winter of 1914–1915 did nothing to help matters.

ABOVE
Smoke emerges from a recently fired French 220mm mortar. Trench warfare on the Western Front demanded heavy guns more suitable to sieges than to mobile warfare, and obsolete weapons such as this one were brought back into service to lob their heavy shells on enemy positions.

RIGHT
A French officer observes the fall of shot using a periscope. Snipers came into their own in trench warfare, as they were able to lay their guns accurately on enemy positions. Except during an assault, when many targets were presented, it was very dangerous to show one's head over the parapet. Periscopes such as this were invaluable to give some idea of what was going on over the other side.

LEFT
The one major offensive carried out by the Germans in 1915 was made in the Ypres sector in April 1915. Poison gas was used for the first time, and proved a considerable success. However, the novelty of the new weapon rapidly wore off, and the British and French launched several counter-attacks during May and June. Here, a June attack along the Messines Road sees the British using a prominently displayed flag to signal back to their own trenches that they had successfully occupied the German front line.

ABOVE
On the Eastern Front, trench warfare was not the fixed affair that it was in the West. Trench defences were temporary matters and the wider area in the fighting zone left more vulnerable, open flanks to exploit. Here, some Austrian soldiers collect rifles from the dead in a captured Russian trench.

ABOVE
RMS *Lusitania* was sunk by the German submarine U-20 on 7 May 1915. Over a thousand people lost their lives as the ship went down in a mere 18 minutes (compared with over two hours for the *Titanic*). Of the dead, 128 were Americans, which helped rouse anti-German sentiment in the USA, already upset over the treatment of the Belgians.

THE WAR AGAINST THE TURKS

Turkey entered the war on the side of Germany and Austria-Hungary in October 1914. The Germans had long cultivated Turkey as an ally for its possible support in threatening the Suez Canal, controlled by the British, and its ability to block passage through the Dardanelles strait between the Aegean and Black Seas, and thus prevent the supply of munitions to the Russians. The Russian army experienced a severe shell shortage throughout 1915, which contributed to heavy defeats on the Eastern Front. One possible solution was seen in seizing the Dardanelles to reopen the supply route and possibly knock Turkey out of the war. The British First Lord of the Admiralty, Winston Churchill, argued for just such a stroke. At first he proposed doing it with ships alone, but then won support for landings. The resulting Gallipoli campaign proved to be a shrewd plan condemned to failure by dreadful execution.

ABOVE
V beach, seen from SS *River Clyde*, on the morning of the initial landings on 25 April 1915. The landings were at first a great success, as Turkish defences were weak, but the British commanders did not move inland aggressively, and the allied forces became trapped on the tip of the Gallipoli peninsula when the Turks rushed troops into blocking positions.

ABOVE
Two Australians guard a well-camouflaged Turkish sniper. Gallipoli did a lot to establish an Australian national identity, as the ANZAC (Australian and New Zealand Army Corps) played a prominent role in the battle. When the campaign was abandoned in January 1916, with a skilful withdrawal from the beaches, the Anzacs had established a reputation as tough fighters.

ABOVE

British guns are ferried across marshes on the Tigris river. The two rivers that give Mesopotamia its name, the Tigris and the Euphrates, required the British to build up a large fleet of shipping suitable for transferring supplies to the troops in the field. By the end of the war the total number of ships available to the British in Mesopotamia approached 2,000, the largest such riverine fleet then in existence.

LEFT

A forward observation officer of the 82nd Battery, Royal Field Artillery, observes the fall of shot during the advance on Kut in the autumn of 1915. As well as the Gallipoli landings, 1915 saw the British launch a campaign in Mesopotamia, which met with initial success. The Turks, however, reorganized and their counter-attack was one of the worst defeats in British military history up to that time, when 10,000 troops at Kut surrendered to the Turks on 29 April 1916.

JUTLAND

While it was thought before the war that the German and British navies would engage in a major naval battle in the North Sea early on in the conflict, in fact it took nearly two years for the main battle fleets to engage the other side. Some skirmishing between them occurred in 1914 and 1915, most notably at the battle of Dogger Bank in January 1915, when a substantial German squadron was beaten by a larger British one. The Germans did decide in May 1916 to risk a battle, hoping to engage a portion of the British fleet before the remainder could intervene. The battle of Jutland, on 31 May–1 June 1916 was the decisive naval engagement of the war. At one point in the battle it looked as if the Germans had in fact succeeded. But in spite of heavy losses, the British fleet succeeded in outmanoeuvering the Germans, who retired, leaving British control of the sea confirmed.

RIGHT

Winston Churchill, when First Lord of the Admiralty, described Grand Fleet commander Admiral Sir John Jellicoe as "the only man who could lose the war in an afternoon". Jellicoe was well aware of this and handled his ships carefully in the battle with the Germans. He has never quite received the credit he deserved for winning the battle of Jutland.

ABOVE
Frederick Rutland stands on the float of his Short 184 seaplane. Rutland flew a reconnaissance mission during the Battle of Jutland from HMS *Engadine*, a seaplane carrier, in one of the first acts of air reconnaissance at sea during a naval battle. However, none of his radio messages locating German ships were passed on. Poor visibility put an end to seaplane flights during the battle after Rutland returned to the *Engadine* with petrol-line problems.

ABOVE
Three British battle cruisers sail in a line ahead formation on the morning of 31 May. The battle cruisers' job was to sail ahead of the main battle fleet and locate the principal enemy force. On this occasion, it brought them into a heavy engagement with their German counterparts. The ship nearest the camera, HMS *Queen Mary*, exploded at 16:26, after being struck by seven German rounds, one of which apparently detonated the forward magazine.

ABOVE
Around 18:30, flames engulf HMS *Invincible* as her forward magazine explodes following an earlier explosion in her central magazine. The British battlecruisers suffered heavily during the engagement, but drew the Germans on towards the main British fleet. The Germans were twice forced to put their whole fleet about to avoid being trapped at the mercy of the broadsides of British battleships. Jellicoe tried hard to place his fleet between the Germans and their base at Kiel, but the Admiralty in London failed to pass on important intercepted radio traffic and the Germans escaped in a confused night action.

ABOVE
The body and helmet of a French soldier lie beside a German infantryman in a ruined trench near Fort Vaux, outside Verdun. Some 675,000 casualties were lost in the battle, and losses on either side were about even. Falkenhayn had sought to make the French suffer disproportionately, but the dogged French defence and their perseverance in attack throughout the autumn made the Germans pay heavily for any gains.

THE 1916 CAMPAIGNS

The year 1916 was the watershed year of the war. Battles at Verdun, the Somme and the Brusilov offensive in the East seemed for no benefit, as no army gained any significant advantage. Each was an attempt to shift the strategic situation dramatically. None achieved anything remarkable except the death of large numbers of soldiers. Verdun, at least, was honestly conceived as a battle of attrition. The German commander von Falkenhayn believed the French would be "bled white". However, the plan miscarried, as the battle dragged on from Feburary to December. The "Big Push" on the Somme in summer 1916 was designed to relieve the pressure on the French, as the British threw their New Armies of 1914–1915 volunteers into action. However, some 600,000 French and British soldiers perished in pushing the German lines back perhaps five miles. The Brusilov offensive resulted in a million casualties, and dislodged the Austro-Hungarian army from its gains of 1915. It also made the Russian Revolution inevitable.

ABOVE

One of the reasons the Germans chose to attack at Verdun was because their railway access to the front lines was far superior to that of their opponents. The French had to rely for supplies instead on *la Voie Sacrée* (the Sacred Way), a road running into Verdun that was under fire from the Germans for much of its length. Trucks ran in a steady stream in both directions bringing supplies to the French defenders and taking away the casualties.

ABOVE
French soldiers serve a 65mm mountain gun in a well-constructed trench battery. Smaller-calibre artillery played a vital role during the war in breaking up attacks by bringing the enemy's forward trenches under fire. It also offered supporting fire to cover friendly advances.

BELOW

British anti-aircraft gunners rush to their 13-pounder gun in March 1916. The effectiveness of aerial reconnaissance led to countermeasures being taken. Airplanes by now mounted machine guns to fire at opposing aircraft, while on the ground machine guns and smaller-calibre artillery were deployed on special mountings to fire shrapnel on timed fuses that exploded, hopefully, in the vicinity of enemy aircraft.

LEFT
Well equipped men of the 4th battalion, the Worcestershire Regiment, on their way to the front for the Somme offensive. The soldier in the foreground has a pair of wirecutters for breaking through barbed wire obstacles. The British forces that massed for the attack represented a genuine "nation in arms", as all had volunteered enthusiastically to fight for King and country. Many battalions, nicknamed Pal's battalions, were drawn from single localities, which was to have tragic effects when the casualty notices began to arrive.

ABOVE
A British soldier stands watch in a captured trench near Orvillers in July, while some of hiscomrades sleep around him. The British attack was preceded by a lengthy bombardment, to demolish the German trenches. However, the bombardment was not as effective as it appeared from a distance. Crossing the great width of the area between the front lines, known as No Man's Land, gave the German defenders time to emerge from shelters and open fire to cut down the lines of advancing British soldiers, among whom casualties on the first day alone reached 60,000.

ABOVE
The most influential fighter aeroplane of the war was the Fokker Eindecker. It utilized a single machine gun synchronized by means of an interruptor gear to fire through the propeller arc. This was an unexpected technical development, and gave the Germans a dramatic advantage from its introduction in May 1915 until new French and British aircraft entered the fray in spring 1916. The reputations of German aces such as Oswald Boelcke and Max Immelmann were established in this type of aircraft.

ABOVE
French soldiers proudly display British military decorations they have received. The French army had by now abandoned the dark blue and red uniform of the opening year of the war. Instead, a pale blue known as *horizon bleu* offered better camouflage on the battlefield, although it was still not as good as the British khaki or the German Feldgrau. The French also adopted the Adrian helmet, a far more elegant design than the British "tin hat".

OVERLEAF
One of the photographs that have provided a key image of the First World War shows 8-inch howitzers of the 39th Siege Battery, Royal Garrison Artillery, bombarding German lines in August 1916. Such heavy field pieces were devastating to the Germans, who suffered losses just as heavy as the British in the Somme battle. The expenditure of ammunition in the Somme bombardments was prodigious. Some 1.6 million rounds were fired during the week-long barrage preceding the opening of the attack on 1 July 1916, equivalent to 16 rounds every minute, day and night.

ABOVE
A still from the famous film *The Battle of the Somme* shows a British front-line machine gun position during a lull in the fighting. The film was intended by the War Office to boost morale on the home front, but its true-to-life scenes of death in battle and the grimness of trench warfare horrified the audience in Britain. It was one of the most counter-productive pieces of propaganda in history.

ABOVE
Tanks were first used at the battle of Flers-Courcelette in September 1916, as part of the Somme offensive. Every single tank then available, 49 in total, was deployed in the attack. Only 15 actually crossed into No Man's Land, the rest falling victim to mechanical unreliability. Even in such small numbers they proved quite effective as the attack gained over a mile of ground, a dramatic advance for the Somme campaign. Field Marshal Sir Douglas Haig, the commander of the British Expeditionary Force, asked for a thousand more.

SUBMARINE WARFARE

Before the war the focus of the naval arms race between Britain and Germany had been on the big battleships and battle cruisers. But the most significant innovation of the naval war was the use of submersible warships. The most dramatic incident in the early days of the war occurred in September 1914 when the *U-9* sank three British cruisers. However, German naval officers soon realized that submarines could also be very effective as commerce raiders. At first the Germans followed formal prize rules, by stopping merchant ships and inspecting their cargoes for contraband. If such cargo was found, the ship's crew would be ordered into lifeboats and the ship sunk.

However, from February 1915 onwards the Germans imposed a system of unrestricted submarine warfare in British waters, allowing U-boats to sink on sight with torpedoes. The United States was outraged, and German U-boats were withdrawn from British waters in September. In October 1916, when the war seemed a stalemate, they returned. In February 1917 restrictions were lifted again. The Germans decided to risk war with the United States in the hope of imposing a blockade on Britain.

ABOVE LEFT
A U-boat torpedoes a merchant ship in the Mediterranean in 1916. Between October 1916 and April 1917, German submarines sank nearly 3 million tons of shipping in the Atlantic and British waters alone. Britain was in serious danger of being cut off from its trade routes, and was thought to have but six weeks' supplies of food remaining.

ABOVE
A British convoy zig-zags in the Atlantic. The only effective countermeasure against the U-boat proved to be the convoy system, which the British Admiralty was reluctant to employ, until the heavy losses in April 1917 convinced them to try it. Sinkings immediately dropped by about one-third. By war's end, 99 per cent of all merchant ships sailing to or from Britain successfully reached their destinations. The convoy, together with superior submarine detection measures and weapons such as the depth charge, had won the U-boat war.

THE BREAKING OF NATIONS

In 1917, the glacial stalemate of 1916 finally showed signs of cracking. Military incompetence and consequent heavy casualties caused the tsarist regime in Russia to collapse in March 1917. In its place came a provisional government that, while still committed to the war, confronted a burgeoning left-wing political movement that called for peace. In April 1917, the United States declared war on Germany, offering a huge reservoir of manpower and its considerable industrial might to the Allied cause. The French army experienced a severe mutiny after a failed offensive, and was no longer the confident force that had managed to save Verdun. Food shortages were already having an effect on the German people, as diseases related to inadequate diet began to rise dramatically in frequency. In Britain, strikes in industry began to occur with regularity. By the end of the year, Russia had been knocked out of the war by a left-wing revolution, releasing half a million German troops for operations on the Western Front. This offered Germany a last chance of a decisive victory, before the impact of US entry into the war and the blockade eroded the German war effort.

ABOVE LEFT
Canadian machine gunners deploy their weapons during the Vimy Ridge battle. The operation was part of a series of attacks by Haig's British Expeditionary Force to divert German attention from the impending French attack on the Aisne. The Canadian operation was an impressive display of coordination, including a well-supplied artillery fire plan that utilized contact fuses to considerable effect.

ABOVE
A forward observation team watches artillery fire during the fighting around Arras in April 1917. Field telephones played an important role that in later wars would be filled by radios. The observers watched the fall of shot and then reported corrections to the firing guns. Once ranged in, a battery could switch to rapid fire and completely destroy the target.

LEFT
British and Australian soldiers study a model of the terrain around Messines Ridge. This was part of the careful preparations made by the commander of the operation, General Sir Herbert Plumer. It was a meticulously-planned operation with limited objectives and a lengthy bombardment that unleashed 3.5 million shells over 12 days, and which relied on the detonation of several mines before the attack went in. It was the largest artificial explosion in human history up to that point, and was heard as far away as London.

ABOVE
Food shortages and military failure fuelled a revolutionary movement in Russia based on workers' and soldiers' Soviets (councils). In March, all military units were ordered to elect deputies to their Soviets. However, a provisional government kept the country in the war. Authority was divided between the government and bureaucracy and the Soviets, which was a recipe for further problems. In November, the Bolsheviks, a Marxist group led by Vladimir Lenin, seized power in a coup and took Russia out of the war. A treaty was signed with Germany in March 1918.

RIGHT
Germany had begun bombing Britain from the air using Zeppelin airships in 1915. In 1917, long-range, twin-engine Gotha bombers such as this replaced the Zeppelins. The aeroplane carried a 1000 lb bomb load, and flew from bases in Flanders. The Germans carried out a total of 27 Gotha raids during the war.

LEFT
On 7 July 1917, the Central Telegraph Office in London was hit and set on fire during a Gotha raid. This was the last daylight raid on London, although there were others in August on Southend and Ramsgate. Subsequent raids were conducted at night, which were less accurate but even harder to defend against. The British made great efforts to do so against the Gothas, deploying anti-aircraft artillery and fighters to intercept them, but these measures were not effective until the London Air Defence Area was set up in August 1917.

LEFT
A victim of shell shock sits in a well-constructed dug-out which served as an Advanced Dressing Station during the fighting around Ypres in Belgium in the summer and autumn of 1917. This battle was fought in far more dreadful weather than the Somme offensive of the previous summer, with heavy rains in August and October turning the ground into a quagmire. The last phase of the fighting revolved around the village of Passchendaele, which in the English-speaking world came to symbolize the total futility of trench warfare.

THE MIDDLE EAST AT WAR

War has always attracted certain kinds of romantics. The ugly mess of the Western Front offered barren soil for romance, which in contrast flourished in the sunshine of the Middle East. Here, in the Arab peoples, who had for centuries been ruled by alien Ottoman masters, the British saw an opportunity to strike at the Turks. Arab nationalism had been percolating in the Middle East for some years. After the Turks launched an attack through the Sinai Peninsula that carried them almost to the Suez Canal, the British turned to the Sherif of Mecca, Hussein, as a figurehead around whom to build an Arab revolt. The key British liaison with the Arabs was T. E. Lawrence, a pre-war archaeologist and wartime intelligence officer, who had won the loyalty of the Arabs through adopting their customs and clothes. While a conventional British Army advanced against the Turks from Egypt, Lawrence molded the Arab tribes into a guerrilla army that attacked Turkish supply lines. Steady pressure from the spring of 1917 onward gradually pushed the Turks from Palestine and even out of Syria.

ABOVE

Lawrence demonstrated the value of his guerrilla army, which was initially regarded as something of a joke, by the daring capture of Aqaba, an important supply base for the Turkish army in Arabia, on 6 July 1917.

ABOVE
"Lawrence of Arabia" was a powerful image, and very much the creation of the shrewd self-promoter in Lawrence, assisted by the American Lowell Thomas (right). Lawrence was extremely diplomatic with the Arabs and convinced them that the British were their friends. In fact, the British had no intention of creating the kind of Arab state Lawrence spoke about, but planned to divide the Middle East with France, and offer a national home for the Jews in Palestine. Lawrence had some knowledge of these plans all along, but kept it to himself.

ABOVE
British cavalry at Kirkuk, Mesopotamia, in May 1918. The initial British campaign in Mesopotamia, which ended in disaster at Kut in April 1916, was followed by a more successful campaign that began at the end of the year. The British successfully pushed the Turks back and captured Baghdad, before the summer heat put an end to the campaign. The war in Mesopotamia continued in a fairly desultory fashion through 1918, as the British advanced in the spring and autumn, and by the end of the war approached Mosul.

RIGHT
Indian soldiers firing rifle grenades in Mesopotamia. The British army in Mesopotamia drew most of its manpower from India. The First World War contributions of the "white dominions" of Canada, Australia, New Zealand and South Africa have frequently been seen as contributing to building those countries' national identities, but India sent more soldiers than any of them.

THE YEAR OF VICTORIES

The loss of Russia to the Allied cause created a race. The Germans were now able to shift a substantial number of reinforcements from the Eastern Front to the Western. If deployed effectively, these could conceivably deliver a knockout blow to the British and French armies. That had to occur before American troops began arriving in France in large numbers, because Germany's war leaders knew that the country would not stand for the war stretching on for much longer. So Germany risked all in a series of spring offensives that aimed at achieving a decisive breakthrough against the British. The three assaults all followed roughly the same pattern. The Allied line gave way and dramatic advances were achieved. But then reinforcements stabilized the position, while the German troops were unable to sustain the attacking vigour of the first few days. In August, an Allied counter-offensive at Amiens and Montdidier delivered a crushing blow to the German army. Constantly keeping up the pressure throughout the autumn, the Allies steadily pushed the Germans back. The trench deadlock had been broken. A starving Germany sued for peace, and the war came to an end on 11 November 1918.

LEFT

German assault troops (*Stosstruppen*) advance rapidly during the spring of 1918. Men such as these were the key to the German successes. They travelled light, carrying only what was needed for the assault. Their tactics of bypassing strong points and driving into the enemy's rear echelon in order to disrupt communications and supplies foreshadowed the blitzkrieg tactics associated with the Germans in the Second World War.

RIGHT
British soldiers perform their toilet in a shell hole near Ypres in September 1918. The German offensives and the Allied counter-offensives restored a level of mobility to the Western Front that had been absent since 1914. Although troops still dug in during battles, trenches were now hasty affairs and a shell hole would serve as a practical ad hoc dugout.

BELOW
The aftermath of the raid on Zeebrugge shows the sunken block ships *Intrepid*, *Iphigenia* and *Thetis* in the canal. The British raid was an attempt to stop the Germans from using the Flanders port as a base for U-boat operations. The plan failed, as the block ships were incorrectly positioned. The raid was a daring idea, and in spite of its failure served as a model for commando operations in the Second World War.

ABOVE
HMS *Argus*, shown here painted in zebra camouflage, was the world's first aircraft carrier to have a flight deck along the entire length of the hull. She was converted from the hull of an Italian passenger liner, which was being built in Britain at the war's outbreak. Her design set the pattern for all future aircraft carriers, enabling wheeled aircraft to take off and land using the full length of the flight deck. The camouflage pattern was intended to make her harder to target from the periscope of a submarine.

ABOVE
US soldiers operate a French-designed 75mm field gun during the autumn 1918 offensives. The American army had to use a lot of equipment supplied from French and British sources, including British helmets and French airplanes. There was also some question of whether the US troops would be deployed as an independent army under American command, or to reinforce existing British and French formations. The American demand to serve under their own commanders was eventually accepted, although during the crisis of spring 1918 American troops did reinforce threatened sectors at brigade and divisional strengths.

OVERLEAF
British troops march through liberated Lille, France, in October 1918. By war's end, the British army was probably the most effective of the Allied forces. Its artillery was the most effective at counter-battery fire, and its intelligence department was markedly superior to that of the Germans. The British use of tanks was the most advanced of all armies, although these were still extremely unreliable vehicles and by no means the war-winners they have sometimes been portrayed as. Co-ordination with the newly created Royal Air Force for reconnaissance purposes was also practised to the highest degree.

LEFT
Allied officers stand outside the railway carriage at Compiègne, where armistice negotiations began on 8 November 1918. Marshal Foch, the Allied Supreme Commander, stands second from right. Hostilities ceased six hours after an armistice was signed, at 11.00am on 11 November.

ABOVE
France celebrates the end of the war on Bastille Day, 1919, beneath the Arc de Triomphe in Paris. The French would have liked the final peace treaty, signed at Versailles on 28 June 1919, to have encompassed more than it did, but Britain and the United States thought even that went too far. Adolf Hitler would prove the French were right.

THE INTERWAR YEARS

1918–1939

The First World War produced dramatic changes both within Europe and in the wider world. Germany's colonial empire was swept away. The Tsarist regime was supplanted by a Soviet one whose ideology threatened the traditional ruling classes of other states, and also their hold over their colonies. The Turkish empire ceased to exist, and the Middle East was reorganized and divided between Britain and France. The United States retreated immediately after war's end into an isolationism that left it a shadowy force in global power politics. Yet it became thereafter an increasingly key military and diplomatic player in world affairs. In such unsettled circumstances, war thrives and many smaller conflicts erupted as diplomatic power ebbed and flowed around the world.

The years between the two world wars were ones in which the major armies digested the lessons of the Great War, and developed weapons that took advantage of technical improvements that had occurred between 1914 and 1918. The increasing availability of radio communication was exploited, as was the greater power offered by tank and aircraft engines.

Technical developments also fed into the visual record of war. The interwar years saw easily portable cameras become widespread, while the importance of photographs in the print media and of the newsreel in cinemas also grew. A category of "war photographers" arose in the late 1930s, whose work was marketed to newspapers around the world. The idea of managing the media began to supplant previous attitudes towards the reporting of war, in which the correspondent or photographer was seen as an intruder. More opportunities were given to photographers by governments and armed forces.

LEFT
Arabs in Iraq on the march in the 1920s. They were opposed to the British mandate over the territory.

THE RUSSIAN CIVIL WAR

The October 1917 Revolution in Russia took the country out of the First World War, but spawned a four-year conflict of its own. Opponents of the new regime took up arms, whether conservatives seeking to re-establish something like the old tsarist order, nationalists hoping to gain independence from Russia, or those trying to check the Bolsheviks' determination to establish a "dictatorship of the proletariat" in their own image. The opponents of the Bolsheviks became generally known as "Whites" and were led largely by former tsarist officers, in contrast to the "Reds" of Bolshevik Moscow. The Whites' initial attempts in 1918 to topple the Reds failed owing to a lack of effective manpower or supplies. However, they received support from the former allies of Russia in the war – Britain, France, the United States and Japan – which increased the military effectiveness of their forces. The period from March to November 1919 saw the near-overthrow of the Bolshevik regime, but a reorganization of the army drove back the Whites, who had reduced Bolshevik control to a relatively small – but well populated and industrialized – area of European Russia around Moscow. Success against the Whites was followed by a war with the newly established independent Polish Republic. However, a lack of co-ordination between the Russian commanders led to the defeat of the Red Army in Poland in 1920. By this stage, the Whites had been largely driven out of Russia, and during 1921 the Bolsheviks re-established their authority over most of the area formerly ruled by the tsars.

RIGHT

Bolshevik soldiers gather around a field kitchen during the Russian civil war. That "an army marches on its stomach" is a cliché, but reasonable hot food does do much to improve the morale of any army, particularly before a battle. Unsung equipment such as the cooking pot is actually as vital to an army as any weapon.

ABOVE
Soldiers of the Czecho-Slovak Legion man machine-guns aboard an armoured train. Armoured trains featured in conflicts as far back as the American Civil War. They provided fire support to operations along railways. The Czecho-Slovak Legion was allied to the White forces in the war, until they were eventually evacuated from Russia via Vladivostok in 1920.

IRELAND 1919–1923

The Anglo-Irish War that broke out in January 1919 was a guerrilla war to gain the independence of Ireland. It drove the British government to negotiate Dominion status for an Irish Free State. A treaty between the Irish nationalist parliament and Britain was agreed in 1921. Six counties in the north, however, remained part of the United Kingdom. This led to a split in the Irish nationalist movement and the outbreak of civil war in June 1922. The British demanded that the Irish government act to end a rebellion, and the subsequent war was in most respects a continuation of the Anglo-Irish war, with the Free State government acting as a proxy for the British.

ABOVE
Irish artillery, borrowed from Britain, shells Tramway House in Dublin, in July 1922. The Irish Civil War began at the end of June 1922, when the Irish army began attacks on various public buildings occupied by anti-Treaty forces in April.

LEFT
Anti-Treaty soldiers march down Grafton Street, Dublin, in July 1922. They are armed with Lee-Enfield rifles, the standard issue weapon of the British army at the time. Often the only concession the anti-Treaty army made to military status was to don a bandolier. A getaway was consequently always fairly easy to achieve, provided the guerrilla ditched the precious rifle.

ABOVE
Pro-Treaty snipers take up a position on the O'Connor Bridge in Dublin during the street fighting in July 1922. Once Dublin had been secured, the government faced fighting the anti-Treaty forces in other towns and in rural areas. Those anti-Treaty men who had previously been occupying government buildings burned them and took to the guerrilla warfare they had used against the British.

THE RIFF WAR

In 1919, Abd-el-Krim began the establishment of a Republic of the Rif, a region of Morocco inhabited by Berber tribes, but largely ignored by both the administration of the French protectorate of Morocco and the government of Spanish Morocco. In 1921, war broke out between the Spanish and the Riffi, when the Spanish set up a military post in territory claimed by the Rif Republic, but believed by the Spanish to be theirs. The war lasted for five years, and included the defeat of Spanish troops at Annual in July 1921, when some 3,000 Riffi warriors overwhelmed a 13,000-strong Spanish force. In the end, it took a combined force of 250,000 French and Spanish troops a year to defeat the Riffi, and the war ended in 1926.

BELOW
Spanish artillery bombards Riffi positions near Tetuan in 1925. Spain's early defeats led to their reinforcing strongly their army in Morocco, including with tanks. During operations with the French in 1925–1926, they also allegedly made use of mustard gas, dropped from aeroplanes on the Riffi.

THE CHACO WAR

Bolivia and Paraguay were the poorest countries in South America, and both coveted Chaco Boreal, a mixture of arid land and jungle that lay between the lusher eastern half of Paraguay, and Bolivia's main population centres in the Andes. The suspicion that oil was present in the Chaco enhanced the region's appeal, and in 1932 the two countries went to war. Though both deployed aircraft and the Bolivians mobilized tanks, a considerable investment for such poor nations, they inflicted less damage than the harsh nature of the region, which claimed more lives through sickness and thirst. The Bolivian army, in spite of its considerable superiority in all types of equipment, proved incapable of defeating the more mobile, tactically astute Paraguayan forces. A ceasefire brought the conflict to the end in 1935, and a treaty signed in 1938 awarded most of the Chaco to Paraguay.

ABOVE

General Hans Kundt inspects a Bolivian army camp. Kundt had been hired by the Bolivian government before the war to instil some Prussian discipline and German efficiency into the army. Unfortunately, he proved to be a general who ignored all the causes of German victories in the First World War on the Eastern Front (where he had served) and denounced genuine reports by his reconnaissance pilots of impending encirclements of Bolivian forces as hopeless exaggerations.

ABOVE
The wreckage of Bolivian tanks bears testimony to the inappropriateness of mechanized warfare to the Chaco terrain. Parts of the Chaco are jungle, which required infantry to open paths through which the tanks could pass, while the hot daytime temperatures turned the metal vehicles into ovens. Consequently, every tank hatch had to be opened while operational, meaning enemy soldiers could toss grenades inside with relative ease.

THE SPANISH CIVIL WAR

The war originated as a rebellion by conservative and nationalist civilians and army officers against the Republican government of Spain. It foreshadowed the Second World War in many respects, both politically and militarily, and drew in both Italian and German intervention on the side of the rebels, while the Republicans received substantial support from the Soviet Union. The war began with an uprising intended to seize many of the important cities of Spain. Had this succeeded, the fighting would almost certainly have been brief. However, the Republicans retained control of Madrid and Barcelona, which gave them an industrial and political base from which to mount a serious war effort. Within a few days, both sides were in control of clearly defined areas of Spain. The remainder of the war saw the gradual squeezing of the Republican area, until the Nationalist rebels finally triumphed in spring 1939. The war clearly prefigured the clash of ideologies that would characterize the Second World War.

ABOVE
A Robert Capa photograph shows Republican militia rushing forwards in an attack in 1936. The amateurish nature of Republican military forces in the war contributed to their failures on the battlefield. The Nationalists, by contrast, could draw on most of the pre-war Spanish army for their forces.

ABOVE
Tanks of the German Condor Legion advance into combat. The German support for the Nationalists was invaluable. German aircraft airlifted Spanish troops from Morocco to Spain, which provided possibly the decisive advantage in securing the success of the Nationalist uprising. The Germans also studied carefully much of what they experienced in the Spanish Civil War, which stood them in good stead in the initial campaigns of the Second World War.

ABOVE
Nationalist infantry occupy a farm wall during an engagement in the summer of 1936. The initial stage of the war was marked by "columns" advancing from Nationalist or Republican enclaves toward enemy-held sectors. Both sides murdered their opponents with impunity as they advanced.

ABOVE

The ruins of the Basque town of Guernica after the German bombing in April 1937. It was market day, and civilian casualties were consequently very high, with over 1,500 people killed and nearly a thousand wounded. The incident became a symbol of the brutality of modern war in general, and of the Nationalists in particular.

LEFT
Nationalist soldiers guard Republican prisoners. The Nationalists regarded the war as an exercise in "purification", ridding the country of the opponents of law and order. Tens of thousands were murdered. Prisoners such as these men might be executed, or sent to prisons or labour camps. The massive memorial to the dead of the war, the Valley of the Fallen outside Madrid, was built using 20,000 prisoners condemned to forced labour.

THE SINO–JAPANESE WAR 1937–1945

The European nations who imposed their "Unequal Treaties" on China were joined enthusiastically by China's neighbour, Japan, at the end of the nineteenth century. The Japanese viewed China as a reservoir of natural resources and as a vital market to be captured for its industrial goods. In the 1920s the Japanese conceived a long-term objective of dividing China into smaller states. In 1931, a short war with China led to the creation of just such a regime in Manchuria, known as Manchukuo. In July 1937, following a shooting incident between Japanese and Chinese troops in Peking, a full-scale war broke out. Initially, Japan achieved major successes, as both its army and navy were far superior to the Chinese forces. However, the size of China and growing support for the Chinese from Western nations, slowed down the Japanese conquest. By 1938, the Japanese had been fought to a stalemate. Although they continued to win battles against the Chinese field armies, a sustained guerrilla campaign prevented the Japanese from employing their forces fully in further conquests. The conflict was absorbed into the Second World War in December 1941. It was marked by all the characteristics of a racial war, with brutal slaughter of Chinese civilians by the Japanese.

LEFT
Japanese soldiers march through a Chinese town. In spite of being substantially outnumbered by the Chinese army, the Japanese succeeded in capturing most important cities on or near the coast during the first year of the war. The Chinese war effort was hampered by the breakdown of the Nationalist regime's alliance with the Chinese Communists led by Mao Tse-tung in late 1938, just at the time the war reached a stalemate.

BELOW
Japanese artillery fires on Chinese positions during the battle for Nanking in late 1937. The capture of the city on 13 December 1937 was followed by six weeks of slaughter, as Japanese troops indiscriminately murdered civilians, including children, and raped women. The actual death toll has been the subject of considerable academic debate, with the lowest estimates amounting to 10,000 and the highest some 350,000. Whatever the total, it was a despicable act.

THE SECOND WORLD WAR

1939–1945

The Second World War was the greatest conflict in human history. From a European perspective, it began with Nazi Germany's invasion of Poland on 1 September 1939. In an important sense, it was merely a continuation of the First World War. The impetus came from Germany, whose dictator, Adolf Hitler, regarded the Versailles settlement as the theft of Germany's rightful victory in eastern Europe. However, the conflict had wider sources than just this. It was, in part, a three-way ideological conflict between capitalism, communism, and a racialist nationalism that had been emerging in Europe even before the First World War. It was also an attempt to answer the question of who would dominate Europe: Russia, Germany or Britain. It arose, too, out of tensions caused by long-standing questions of national self-determination in central and eastern Europe. And it was also concerned with the global balance of power between Europe and the United States.

But for the majority who experienced the war, such issues were almost meaningless. The suffering was immense. Millions were killed in its battles, in bombing raids on cities, in death camps set up to murder European Jews, and by other effects of war such as hunger and disease.

The war advanced technology. Most dramatically, it unleashed the power of the atom. However, great strides were also made in electronics, in communications and other scientific and technical fields.

It was also a media war. The art of war photography reached new heights, as cameras were now widely available and easily carried. Colour photography, both in moving and still pictures, became widespread and the images of war were widely diffused, as governments mobilized their populations for total war.

LEFT
US Sherman tanks roll through the streets of Palermo.

LEFT
The German foreign minister von Ribbentrop shakes hands with the Soviet leader Joseph Stalin at the signing of the Nazi-Soviet Pact in August 1939. The pact stunned the world, as the two regimes had previously regarded one another as implacable foes. But the capitulation by France and Britain at Munich in 1938 had left the Soviets with little trust in the Western European powers, who in turn had long regarded the Soviet regime with suspicion. Stalin made his own accommodation with the Germans in the hope of buying time and space for his armies to prepare for some future attack by the Germans.

POLAND AND THE PHONEY WAR

The Second World War began with the German invasion of Poland on 1 September 1939. The campaign lasted less than a month. Poland was overwhelmed. The Poles were outnumbered, and fought an army that was better equipped and an air force superior both in numbers and in the quality of its aircraft. They were also attacked by the Soviets. Poland's one hope lay in an effective invasion of Germany by the French and British. But the British army was still largely in Britain, and the French made only a half-hearted move across the German border. When Poland fell, this offensive was abandoned. The war then settled into a period in which little happened. The Germans shifted their forces to the West, the French and British prepared to meet the inevitable German attack in the spring. This period of relative inactivity was so unlike the anticipated war and so unlike the experience of the First World War, that it became known as the Phoney War.

ABOVE
Polish troops, who had been among the defenders of Warsaw, march into captivity on 27 September 1939. Poland was now handed over to German rule, and the Germans made a point of eliminating those members of the Polish elite they could find. The Poles were to be turned into an ill-educated labour force, serving German needs. A Polish government-in-exile was established by some of the leaders who escaped the country, and a Polish army was also formed from soldiers who had managed to cross the country's borders into neutral states. Few of these men would ever return to a free Poland.

ABOVE
French troops on parade in tunnels beneath one of the forts of the Maginot Line. This line of anti-tank obstacles, fortified gun positions and machine gun posts, named after the French defence minister who was in office when the construction began, has acquired a reputation as a wasted effort. However, the Germans never contemplated attacking through the line, which considerably reduced the area the French needed to concentrate their army in. In that sense the Maginot line was a complete success. However, Charles de Gaulle, among several others, opposed their construction, believing the money would be better spent on an armoured force.

BELOW

French gunners fire a 75mm field gun. The quick-firing recoil mechanism of this field piece was a key technological breakthrough when it entered service in 1897. The fact that it was still a useful weapon 40 years later was testimony to its excellent design.

OVERLEAF

The burning wreckage of a German warship marks the end of a dramatic episode of the Phoney War – the pursuit of the German cruiser *Graf Spee*. Known popularly as a "pocket battleship", the *Graf Spee* sank nine merchant ships before being caught by three smaller British cruisers off the coast of Uruguay. The British damaged the *Graf Spee*, which put into the port of Montevideo for repairs. Here, a skilful deception operation convinced the German ship's commander, Captain Hans Langsdorff, that the British were about to be heavily reinforced. Instead of risking the loss of his ship in battle, Langsdorff scuttled her in the River Plate.

ABOVE
The crewman of a British bomber pushes leaflets out during a flight over Germany. At the outbreak of war, the Royal Air Force believed that the bombing of cities would have a terrible effect on the civilian population and on war industries. However, after a daylight raid against the German navy in September 1939 produced only heavy losses, Bomber Command restricted much of its efforts to dropping leaflets ("nickelling"). The British government clung to a belief, against all evidence, that the Germans could be convinced to revolt against the Nazis, and wasted time, money and effort pursuing this chimera.

HITLER TRIUMPHS IN THE WEST

The Germans welcomed the Phoney War, for it gave them time to prepare their own attack. Initially, they planned a repeat of the Schlieffen Plan the Germans had used at the outset of the First World War. The main weight of the German advance would push through northern Belgium, aiming at seizing the Channel ports. However, an enterprising staff officer named Erich von Manstein suggested an alternative plan involving sending a powerful tank and armoured thrust through the Ardennes, crossing the Meuse between Dinant and Sedan, and advancing to the coast. Hitler adopted this plan, which caught the French totally by surprise. They had committed too much of their strength to confronting the anticipated thrust through northern Belgium to be able to recover in time to halt the German advance. The attack, launched on 10 May 1940, delivered total victory over France by 22 June.

ABOVE
German soldiers disembark on the Norwegian coast on 9 April 1940. Prior to the attacks on the Low Countries and France, the Germans had invaded Denmark and Norway. The main objective was to protect Sweden, the main source of German iron ore, against attack from the west. Denmark fell easily, but Norway proved more difficult to conquer. The Norwegians resisted as fiercely as they could. The Germans lost the heavy cruiser *Blücher* and, after initial success. were driven out of Narvik, the main port for exporting Swedish ore, by British ships and British and French troops. However, the Anglo-French expeditionary force could not hold the city in the face of German occupation of the country and the Germans recaptured the port on 9 June.

RIGHT
German airborne troops celebrate after the capture of the Belgian fortress at Eben Emael on 11 May 1940. The Germans had already performed the first parachute drop in the history of war during the invasion of Norway a month earlier. The capture of Eben Emael, using gliders, was another first. The gliders landed directly on top of the fort, thereby allowing the Germans to minimize the effects the interlocking fields of fire between the fort's gun emplacements and machine gun ports would have had on a more conventional attack.

ABOVE
The French destroyer *Bourrasque* sinks after striking a mine during the operation to evacuate French and British troops from Dunkirk. Over 330,000 troops were rescued between 26 May and 4 June 1940 as German aircraft attempted to halt the evacuation by bombing beaches and ships. For Britain, every available ship from the ports in the south took part. British and French naval vessels also participated.

THE BATTLE OF BRITAIN

With France defeated by the Germans, only Britain remained in the way of Hitler's being able to turn against the Soviet Union without needing to worry about an invasion in the West. Attacking Britain, however, was a difficult proposition. The army needed to cross the English Channel. The German navy lacked the strength to protect an invasion fleet against the Royal Navy. This left the German air force to find some way of tilting the balance in Germany's favour. Its commander, Reichsmarschall Hermann Göring, was delighted to demonstrate that his service could win the war for Germany. The battle was launched on 12 August 1940. Initially, the Germans attacked Britain's air defences and the battle hung in the balance. However, the Germans were suffering heavier losses than the British in both bombers and fighters, and by the end of the month chose to shift the focus of their attacks to London. Because of the short flying range of the German fighters, bomber losses escalated as German fighters could spend but ten minutes over London before having to retire. The German air force now gave up any hope of seizing control of the air and on 19 September the German invasion was postponed indefinitely. The British had won the first major victory over the Germans.

ABOVE
This Chain Home radar station was part of the first line of Britain's air defence. The Chain Home stations were designed to detect high-altitude aircraft formations. The information provided by radar was used by Fighter Command to decide where to direct defending squadrons on intercept courses. The Germans initially targeted the stations, but their steel girder structure made them difficult to knock down, and eventually they gave up the attempt.

ABOVE
Barrage balloons float over a target in Britain. These were cheap and effective methods of rendering bombing ineffective, as aircraft had to fly above the height of the balloons in order to avoid the cables tethering the balloon to the earth. The Germans relied heavily on dive bombing for precision, and barrage balloons prevented such attacks.

RIGHT
A German Heinkel He-111 medium bomber flies over the London docklands on 7 September 1940. Some analysts have argued that the shift of target from Fighter Command airfields to London, made at the beginning of September 1940, was a serious mistake, as the airfields had been at risk of being put out of commission.

ABOVE
Staff officers move symbols representing squadrons across a map of Britain and northern France, as senior officers observe from a gallery in the Operations Room at Fighter Command headquarters. The policy of sending up individual squadrons to subject German bomber formations to continuous attacks was vindicated by the outcome of the battle, although at the time it was a source of controversy.

ABOVE
Lieutenant Karl-Heinz Thruz pilots an He-111 bomber. The He-111 carried the heaviest bomb load of any German aircraft during the battle, at 4,500 lbs. Casualties among pilots on both sides were heavy, but the British were more efficient about replacing such losses. In the end, many German pilots suffered a kind of combat fatigue that was nicknamed "Channel Sickness".

THE MEDITERRANEAN 1941

Italy entered the war in June 1940, with Mussolini declaring war on France and Britain at a point when the war seemed to be won. It might have suited Germany better if he had stayed out. The Italian armed forces were hopelessly mismanaged and inadequately supported by the smallest industrial base of any of the so-called Great Powers. The Italian army in Libya attacked the British in Egypt in September 1940; and was routed in December 1940 and January 1941, requiring German support. The Italian army in Albania attacked Greece (a neutral country) in October 1940; and became bogged down in the mountains in the northwest, until German troops again came to the rescue. The Italian battle fleet was virtually confined to port by the British who, using torpedo planes, managed to knock half their battleships out of action at Taranto in November 1940. The Germans managed to put things right for the Axis by conquering Yugoslavia and Greece, and restoring some equilibrium in North Africa. But it was a diversion of resources the Germans, on the verge of the decisive moment of the war, could perhaps have done without.

RIGHT

A massive column of Italian prisoners heads into captivity during the British counter-attack into Cyrenaica (eastern Libya) in January 1941. The 36,000-strong British Western Desert Force destroyed an Italian army, 250,000 in number, taking 130,000 prisoners, 380 tanks and 845 guns, for the loss of less than 2,000 casualties.

ABOVE
A German 88mm anti-aircraft gun fires at British tanks in April 1941. This gun became the outstanding anti-tank weapon of the war. The Germans reinforced the Italian forces in Libya in February 1941 with what became known as the Deutsches Afrika Korps. Its commander, Erwin Rommel, had made his reputation as commander of the 7th Panzer Division in the French campaign. He reinforced this reputation with his skilful handling of the Italo-German forces during the coming 18 months.

ABOVE

German tanks advance along a Greek railway line in April 1941 Greece to bypass a destroyed road. The Italian invasion of Greece had failed, and the reinforcement of the Greek army with British and Commonwealth troops resulted in the German invasion of Yugoslavia and Greece. The Greeks were defeated and their British support was forced to evacuate the country.

LEFT
German paratroopers make an assault drop on Crete on 20 May 1941. After evacuating Greece, the British had withdrawn part of their force to Crete. The German parachute drop ended in a remarkable success. Although for a moment it looked like the British might have defeated it, they neglected to keep the Germans out of Maleme airfield. Reinforcements were flown in, the Germans achieved air superiority and the British withdrew from the island, suffering heavy losses in the evacuation.

THE BATTLE OF THE ATLANTIC

The Germans' best chance at winning the First World War came when they brought Britain to the brink of starvation through the attacks by their U-boats on British merchant shipping. At the outset of the Second World War, Britain imported two-thirds of her food, 30 per cent of iron ore, 95 per cent of oil and petrol, and 80 per cent of her wool. Figures for other vital war materials were similar. The German navy saw a similar opportunity to that in the First World War and, unlike in the earlier conflict, this time the emphasis of wartime operations would lie in attacks on Britain's seagoing lifeline. This time the Germans co-ordinated U-boat operations more effectively in so-called "wolf-packs" of vessels, strung across the likely routes of convoys. The Atlantic war had its own particular horrors. U-boat attacks often resulted in ships suddenly exploding without warning. Being on a torpedoed ammunition carrier or oil tanker (a popular target) could lead to horrific casualties. An unlucky U-boat became a sunken coffin. The Atlantic was also normally too cold to survive for very long should one find oneself in the water. Crews of both U-boats and escorts had little privacy, and rough waters could make for unpleasant sailing.

ABOVE LEFT

A convoy forms up for sailing in a British port. The British have remembered their hard-learnt lessons from the last war. The convoy system was instituted immediately, and efforts to expand the escort force were put in hand straightaway.

ABOVE

The crew of a Coastal Command aircraft signal a ship below. Aircraft played an important role for both sides. The Germans had some long-range aircraft, which had a measure of success bombing or torpedoing merchant ships but not enough to make a major difference. Anti-submarine aircraft were very effective, being difficult to spot and travelling at much higher speeds than the U-boat. The U-boats' main chance at surviving air attack was to submerge within 30 or 40 seconds of sighting an aircraft. Otherwise, they were a fairly easy target.

ABOVE
The German battleship *Bismarck* fires a salvo during the action in the Denmark Strait on 24 May 1941. HMS *Hood* was sunk in the battle with the loss of all but three of its crew of 1,400. The Germans had a small force of surface ships, but they were not nearly as efficient at sinking British merchant ships as the U-boats.

RIGHT
Survivors of the sunken *Bismarc*k are rescued by HMS *Dorsetshire* on 27 May 1941. The pursuit of the *Bismarck* involved most of the major surface units of the Royal Navy. The German battleship was doomed once its steering gear had been damaged by a Fleet Air Arm torpedo attack on 26 May. Two Royal Navy battleships and two heavy cruisers then sunk her after a battle in which they fired some 300 shells. Only 117 survived from the German ship's crew of 2,200.

LEFT
US soldiers on parade in Iceland, in October 1941. In August 1941, US President Franklin Roosevelt and British Prime Minister Winston Churchill agreed to a system of US support for the British in the Atlantic war. The US would provide convoy protection as far as the Mid Ocean Meeting Point south of Iceland. US soldiers had already been stationed in Iceland since July. US escorts were soon engaging German U-boats even though the two nations were ostensibly at peace.

BARBAROSSA

The German invasion of the Soviet Union began on 22 June 1941. The Germans recognized that they had to destroy the Red Army quickly, over the summer, to have any chance of winning the campaign. But Hitler's schemes were far too ambitious for his armed forces. Having crashed across the border, the German forces achieved substantial victories at Bialystok and Minsk in July, Smolensk and Vinnitsa in August, Kiev in September and Vyazma-Bryansk in October. These engagements netted some 1.8 million prisoners, in addition to casualties inflicted. Yet the Red Army numbered some 4.5 million, plus all the reservists who could be mobilized in time of emergency. In October, the Germans launched their final offensive against Moscow. In early December, the spires of the Kremlin were spotted by the leading elements of the German attack, but already Soviet counterattacks had disrupted the German plan. Even if Moscow had fallen, it is hard to see how that would have led to victory. Soviet counter-attacks in December and January drove the Germans back from the capital.

ABOVE

A German PzKpfw III tank of the 18th Panzer division tank surges out of the Bug river during the first days of the invasion. This is an example of a submersible tank, with a degree of waterproofing that allowed to enter water up to 13 feet deep, that was originally developed for use in the invasion of Britain.

ABOVE
A German 50mm anti-tank gun crew engages Red Army tanks during the opening weeks of Barbarossa. As well as capturing millions of Soviet prisoners, the Germans destroyed many of the enemy's 12,000 tanks. However, the large number was deceptive. Many of the tanks destroyed were obsolete and perhaps only a quarter of them were operational. Even of those, only 1,475 were the newer T-34 and KV-1 models.

LEFT
From atop the roof of a Russian house, German forward observers spot the fall of shot. Artillery was the one of the few areas in which the German invaders outnumbered the Russian defenders. German artillery took a little longer to deliver its fire than in the British or American armies and tended to fire smaller numbers of rounds, but from more guns.

ABOVE
Soviet factory equipment travels east from western Russia to new sites in the Urals. The plan to shift all this vital plant plus its workers and staff was drawn up in July 1941, and between August and October some 80 per cent of Soviet industrial capital was moved. Once the machines had arrived at their destinations, they were often put into operation even as the factory was constructed around them.

ABOVE
German officers execute Soviet citizens with pistol shots in the back of the head. Mass executions followed in the wake of the German advance. The usual victims were Communist party officials and Jews. The atrocities committed by the Germans did much to alienate possible support from a population that had experienced a decade of famine and political purges which had sent millions to their graves either through hunger or from overwork in labour camps.

ABOVE
Soviet troops, well equipped with winter-weather clothing, advance during the winter offensives of 1941–1942. The German advance outpaced their supply lines, and priority was given to ammunition and fuel over winter clothes. As the Germans neared Moscow, they found themselves ill-prepared for the freezing weather. However, Stalin threw away the Soviet advantage by demanding an attack all along the front, rather than concentrating his counterblow against the German Army Group Centre outside Moscow.

JAPAN STRIKES

The Japanese offensive against China, launched in 1937, turned into a general war in the Pacific at the end of 1941. The United States, through a system of economic sanctions, gradually drove the Japanese into making a difficult choice between giving up in China or widening the war to one against all the Western imperialist powers. An oil embargo instituted in July 1941 by the United States was the trigger for the Japanese attack, although in October 1940 Japanese national leaders had already begun preparing for war with the United States around a year later. In December 1941, the Japanese struck against the British in Malaya and Burma, the United States in the Philippines, and against the Dutch East Indies. They also attacked the American Pacific Fleet at its main Pearl Harbor base in Hawaii. The Japanese attack caught the world by surprise, and had achieved all its main objectives by the end of February 1942. However, of the world's great powers, Japan had the weakest industrial base of all except Italy. The Japanese were well aware of this, and their strategy was based on making any counter-offensive so costly that the Western powers would agree to a compromise peace. The opening attacks were merely a means to secure a defensive perimeter far removed from the Japanese homeland.

ABOVE LEFT
On 7 December 1941, smoke billows from the wrecks of American ships on Battleship Row, Pearl Harbor, Hawaii. The Japanese achieved total surprise, in part thanks to the inefficient use of intelligence and radar sightings by the American commanders in Hawaii and the continental United States. Two battleships were destroyed and several others were put out of action. However, no American aircraft carriers were present in the harbour at the time of the attack, an absence that was to prove costly to Japan in the campaigns to come.

ABOVE
The delegation to discuss the surrender of the British army in Malaya meets with its Japanese counterparts on 15 February 1942. From the start, the Japanese portrayed their campaigns as a strike by victims of Western colonialism against their masters, and images such as this helped to support this characterization.

ABOVE
Burmese residents of the town of Tavoy greet Japanese soldiers advancing through the town. This picture belies a reality in Burma where many civilians fled from the approaching Japanese, only to die in the rugged terrain of that southeast Asian country. The Japanese conquest of Burma was complete by May 1942.

1942 – THE TIDE TURNS

In 1942, beginning in June, a succession of campaigns gradually tilted the war away from the Axis powers of Germany, Japan and Italy. In the Pacific, the Japanese attempted to fine-tune their defensive perimeter, with attacks on Port Moresby in New Guinea, Midway Island in the Pacific, and in the Solomon Islands. Each of these efforts was beaten back, in the case of the Battle of Midway incurring heavy losses the Japanese could ill afford. In North Africa, an Italo-German force advanced into Egypt and came close to Cairo. However, the British held firm at a good defensive position at El Alamein, and in October crushed the enemy in a well executed assault masterminded by General Bernard Montgomery, who would become Britain's leading army commander of the war. In the Soviet Union, the Germans seemed to experience the kind of success they had known in 1941, with an advance to the Volga and the Caucasus in the south. However, unlike the previous year, in 1942 the Red Army bided its time, and drew the Germans into a masterfully managed battle in the city of Stalingrad. In November, a Soviet counter-blow shattered the German army, and the strategic initiative on the Eastern Front finally shifted decisively to the Soviets.

ABOVE

The American aircraft carrier USS *Lexington* burns during the Battle of Coral Sea, 7–8 May 1942. The ship sank, but while the engagement was a tactical victory for the Japanese, it was a strategic defeat, since they were forced to abandon an attempt to capture Port Moresby. It was also notable as the first naval battle which, by virtue of both sides using aircraft carriers, took place without ships of either side ever sighting one another.

ABOVE
American Douglas SBD Dauntless dive-bombers in action during the Battle of Midway on 4 June 1942. The Japanese sought to occupy the island, but the Americans, thanks to having broken Japanese naval codes, were able to counter this move by positioning their own aircraft carriers in defence of the island. The battle itself was an illustration of how important luck can be in warfare, given comparable forces. Attacking American aircraft spotted the Japanese carriers at a moment when most of their aircraft were being fuelled and armed. Thus, American bombs detonated the Japanese explosives on deck, and aviation fuel fumes then ignited easily, turning three Japanese aircraft carriers into burning wrecks in minutes.

ABOVE
A platoon of the 4th Indian Division advances under shellfire in the Western Desert. The infantry move at the run and try to avoid bunching up. An officer watches over his men as they go forward, to ensure against straggling. On all fronts infantry tactics were a matter of rushing forward from one area of cover ("defilade") to the next in an attempt to bring enemy positions under small-arms fire.

ABOVE
An American Lease-Lend M3 Grant tank of the Eighth Army trundles past a knocked-out German vehicle. The battle of El Alamein was won through a combination of British artillery and American-supplied tanks, used in co-ordination to minimize losses and to apply overwhelming strength against the enemy. While lacking the elegance of German Blitzkrieg manouevres, these tactics were just as effective in winning battles.

RIGHT
A Women's Royal Naval Service radio mechanic readies herself for a flight. The British did not use women in combat roles, but they did play an important part in ferrying aircraft across the Atlantic and in testing gear before it was issued to fighting units. Indeed, the Allies were far more effective at mobilizing women for the war effort than the Germans and this was one of several factors that tilted the war in their favour in 1942.

ABOVE
British Lancaster bombers make a daylight raid against an armaments factory at Le Creusot, France, 17 October 1942. The Lancaster was a four-engine bomber capable of carrying a massive bomb load of 14,000 lbs. It was the best British strategic bomber of the war and its arrival in service in 1942, together with other big bombers such as the Short Stirling and the Handley-Page Halifax, enabled Bomber Command to launch increasingly powerful night-time air raids against German cities. These involved the questionable practice of "area bombing", in which the district around a legitimate target was saturated with bombs in the hope of hitting the target of the raid, but with no regard for consequent civilian casualties.

ABOVE
US Marines land on Guadalcanal Island in the Solomons on 7 August 1942. The battle for Guadalcanal lasted until February 1943 and involved air, sea and land actions. The Japanese invested much effort in winning the battle, sending reinforcements and naval raids as often as their restricted oil resources would permit. But American superiority in fire-power defeated them on land, while at sea the Japanese could not follow up any successes effectively.

ABOVE
A German soldier walks past casualties of the Dieppe raid on 19 August 1942, including a Churchill tank specially modified for amphibious operations. The attack on Dieppe was of questionable use. It tested some of the ideas the Allies were planning for an eventual assault on France, but at tremendous cost to the largely Canadian force that carried it out. The impact on the Canadian people was comparable to the effects of the Somme offensive in 1916 on Britain – the losses touched whole communities dreadfully.

ABOVE
Rear-Admiral Sir Harold Burrough informs the crew of his ship that they are participants in an Anglo-American operation named *Torch* to invade French North Africa in November 1942. The debate over the "Second Front" against the Germans was waged through early 1942, but in the end the invasion of France was set aside for an operation to open a new front in North Africa.

LEFT
On 8 November 1942, American troops wait in a landing craft en route to their Operation *Torch* landing beaches at Oran in Algeria. The American army was something of an enigma to allies and opponents alike. The army had only recently been expanded from one smaller than the army of Romania. It was certainly a well equipped force, the morale of the troops was very high, and it was very well organized. But it was relatively untested in modern combat and its performance in the First World War had been marked by serious problems related to logistics.

THE STALINGRAD CAMPAIGN

While in 1941 the Germans planned to sweep across the width of the Soviet Union, the losses sustained in that campaign left them with more limited objectives for 1942. This time, the offensive would only take place in the south, and would be aimed at the oil-fields of the Caucasus and the Volga river at Stalingrad. Hitler hoped to repeat the encirclement battles of the previous year, but this time the Red Army showed itself to be more astute and withdrew before the German advance. Hitler came to believe the vast reservoir of Soviet manpower was now exhausted and urged his armies to push forward as far as their supplies would allow. However, at Stalingrad, the Germans found themselves caught in a vicious urban battle. The Red Army, meanwhile, accumulated its reserves and carefully planned its counter-stroke. On 19 November 1942, this was unleashed in a series of pincer assaults that shattered the Axis front and resulted in the encirclement of the German 6th Army at Stalingrad. Desperate German measures to keep this army supplied from the air, while attempting to restore land communications, failed. The last elements of the 6th Army surrendered on 2 February 1943, with the whole campaign costing the Germans and their Allies some 500,000 soldiers.

ABOVE LEFT
A Red Army platoon in training deploys in a textbook firing position, with the soldiers arranged to provide overlapping fields of fire. The Red Army's tactical skills improved with each battle, but this did not always guarantee success. An offensive operation in the spring of 1942 around Kharkov was humiliatingly beaten back by the Germans and the failure made the German advance during the initial stages of the Stalingrad campaign easier.

ABOVE
Trucks take supplies to Leningrad across the frozen Lake Ladoga, a route known as the "Road of Life". While Stalingrad was the decisive battle of the Eastern Front, a prolonged siege of Leningrad, from September 1941 to January 1944, dragged on in the north. Hunger was a constant problem in Leningrad, and even incidents of cannibalism were recorded. The city was the first Soviet municipality to be awarded the title of "Hero City", in recognition of its suffering.

ABOVE

A German soldier hurries across a street among the ruins of Stalingrad. While the streets seem empty, in fact the civilian residents of the city survived hiding where they could – in cellars, in shell holes or in shelters built among the ruins.

ABOVE
German soldiers walk inside the Tractor Plant, scene of some of the heaviest fighting of the Battle of Stalingrad, It took some five German divisions to capture this objective, The battle was carefully managed by the Soviets, who fed a steady supply of replacements into combat – just enough to keep the Germans at bay, but not so many as to delay their build up for a counter-offensive.

THE BOMBING OF GERMANY

The Royal Air Force believed that bombing strategic targets would be its most important contribution to the war effort. However, the inaccuracy of high-altitude level bombing and the heavy casualties suffered on daylight raids rendered the principle invalid. The US Army Air Force faced the same problem in 1943, but in early 1944, large numbers of single-engine fighters, like the P-47 Thunderbolt and the P-51 Mustang, were fitted with drop tanks that extended their range far enough to give cover to bombing missions in Germany. The result was an intense war of attrition that effectively destroyed the German air force.

ABOVE
British Lancaster bombers in flight. The Lancaster was weakly armed with defensive machine guns, with only eight .303-in weapons. But it carried a large bomb-load and adapted Lancasters took part in the famous "Dambusters" raid in May 1943, and also sank the German battleship *Tirpitz*, in November 1944.

RIGHT
German women clear rubble caused by Allied bombing. Raids on German cities led to massive casualties. Operation *Gomorrah*, a series of raids on Hamburg in July and August 1943 killed 50,000 people. A raid on Kassel in October 1943 caused 10,000 deaths. The notorious Dresden raid in February 1945 killed 25,000.

K&S

ABOVE
B-17E bombers of the US Army Air Force fly in their characteristic tight box formation during a raid on Germany in mid-1943. The vapour trails of their fighter escorts appear behind them. The USAAF believed that the much heavier defensive armament of its B-17s (which mounted 11 machine guns), together with the tighter 'box' formations it flew would give its aircraft a better chance of surviving attacks by fighters during unescorted daylight missions. In practice, such missions in 1943 experienced loss rates of 16–20 per cent, a wholly unacceptable level.

KURSK

In the spring of 1943, the Germans held the advantage on the Eastern Front only because the Soviets allowed them to. The Soviet plan was to allow the Germans to attack and then to strike against their over-extended forces. Thanks to an intelligence coup, the Red Army knew the exact whereabouts of the German thrust near the town of Kursk. While the Germans re-equipped with powerful new tanks, the Soviets constructed a belt of defences around Kursk. The battle, launched on 4 July 1943, included the greatest tank combat in history. It ended after nine days. The Germans had suffered very heavy losses, while the Soviets had suffered even more, but they had broken the fangs of the German army in the east. As the German effort halted, the Soviets began a summer offensive along the southern half of the Eastern Front. By December 1943 Germany had lost control of all of the eastern Ukraine, while, the siege of Leningrad was finally raised.

ABOVE
Soviet Field Marshal Georgi Zhukov (pointing) inspects a captured German PzKpfw VI Tiger I tank. The Germans placed much confidence in new models, designed for the Kursk offensive after their tanks were out-classed by the Red Army's T-34. The PzKpfw V Panther, a German copy of the T-34, and the SdKfz 184 Ferdinand tank destroyer were also used.

LEFT
Red Army infantry man a machine gun position. The machine gun is a PM1910 7.62mm Maxim machine gun on a Sokolov wheeled mounting with shield. This venerable design was used by the Russian Imperial Army during the First World War and was still seen in use among Soviet-supported armies in the 1970s.

ABOVE
Soviet 76.2mm field guns deployed for direct fire. The Red Army relied heavily on its artillery, but unlike its German counterpart and its British and American allies' tactics, almost all the artillery shelling was conducted at the outset of any offensive. The idea of artillery as a supporting arm, employed to shell targets of opportunity as the attack unfolded, was not adopted, in part because of the relative paucity of portable radio equipment.

ABOVE
In the foreground, a Soviet field engineer digs a hole for a mine while under German mortar fire. The Kursk defences were elaborate. Over 3,000 miles of trenches were dug, and over 400,000 mines were laid, the latter carefully positioned so as to direct tanks into ideal terrain and under the barrels of some of the 6,000 anti-tank guns. The German attack stood no chance, even if the German army still remained more efficient than its Soviet counterpart.

RIGHT
A Canadian soldier readies a grenade during street fighting in an Italian town. The grenade was an invaluable weapon in such conditions. The blast and resulting shrapnel in an enclosed space was far more likely to be effective than in an open field. In such circumstances, soldiers were very fond of their "pocket artillery".

THE ITALIAN CAMPAIGN

The war in North Africa ended on 13 May 1943 with the surrender of the German and Italian armies there. The Allies' planned invasion of Sicily was launched in July. After that, the British wanted to invade mainland Italy. The Americans were reluctant, but the British prevailed. The Italian campaign was awkward, since the peninsula is thin and contains many easily defended river lines. The initial landings in the late summer of 1943 led to the collapse of the Fascist regime. After hard fighting around Salerno, the next pause occurred along the Gustav line, which included the fiercely defended monastery at Monte Cassino. Rome fell on 5 June 1944, in spite of the setback suffered through a clever but mismanaged amphibious coup at Anzio in January 1944. The next German bastion was the Gothic line, north of Tuscany. The Germans held out for most of the rest of 1944, and mobile warfare, leading to the Germans' final defeat, only resumed the following spring.

ABOVE
British troops cross a pontoon bridge built by US engineers over the Volturno river. The Germans in Italy were highly skilled at demolishing bridges and roads, so the ability to put up temporary structures that would keep the advance going was invaluable.

ABOVE
Polish troops hurl hand grenades during the fight for Monte Cassino in the spring of 1944. It took four battles to drive the Germans out of their strongly defended position. The defenders were paratroopers, their attackers in turn were Americans, Indians, New Zealanders, Poles and French. Until the last battle, the Allied attacks were marked by mistakes bordering on fundamental incompetence.

DEFEAT OF THE U-BOATS

The war against the U-boat is divided into periods, much like geological ages. While the Germans never posed an immediate threat to Britain, as they had in the First World War with the foodstuff shortage their blockade had caused, there were times when pessimism coloured the long-term outlook of British planners. The moments of deepest depression came in the first half of 1941 and the first three months of 1943. Early 1942 was the time of greatest exasperation, as the American refusal to adopt the convoy system for home waters traffic resulted in needless losses. However, moments of German success tended to coincide with times when their coded signals were difficult to break. At times when the code was broken, Allied technological achievements gave them a decisive advantage in the struggle. After April 1943, improved radar, more very-long-range aircraft, direction-finding equipment for detecting radio signals and more efficient deployment of escorts combined to increase U-boat losses. The Germans never recovered the advantage and, from May 1943 to the end of the war, lost more U-boats than they sank merchant ships.

LEFT

American sailors load bombs into a Hedgehog anti-submarine mortar. Sonar (underwater sound detection) did not offer coverage into the forward arc of a ship, and a detected submarine could be lost as the escort navigated towards the target. To compensate for this shortcoming, this British weapon was designed to throw its bombs into the ocean ahead of the bows.

RIGHT
A German U-boat is attacked by Allied bombers in August 1944. The Germans attempted to find technical breakthroughs of their own to cope with Allied advances. The schnorkel, a pipe that allowed air into the submarine and therefore permitted more submerged running, was invaluable in reducing the chance of the submarine's being sighted on the surface. But it was not enough. The U-boat crews suffered the highest loss rate of any arm of service in the Second World War, with casualties amounting to 70 per cent of those who served.

ABOVE
A soldier stands sentry over the 406mm gun emplacement of the Lindemann battery in the Pas de Calais, where Hitler wrongly assumed the Allies would make their main landing.

THE NORMANDY CAMPAIGN

The Allied invasion of France was a topic of intense debate on both sides of the English Channel. "Where would the landing come?" asked the Germans. "When should it be made?" wondered the Allies. When the invasion finally came, in Normandy in June 1944, it provided an illustration of how delay, when a consequence of careful preparation, can in fact be positive. The landings on 6 June 1944 were successful, although the US force landing on the beach code-named Omaha was on the point of being abandoned. The Germans rushed reinforcements to Normandy and gradually both sides built up their strength in and around the beachhead. In spite of unexpectedly tough resistance from the Germans in some quarters, a much slower advance inland than expected, weather problems and heavy casualties, the Allies crossed the Seine river on schedule 90 days after the initial landings, with the Germans in full retreat towards their frontiers. This was in no small measure the result of preparations that involved artificial harbours (the Mulberries), PLUTO (a pipeline for petroleum products under the ocean), a relentless shipping schedule and excellent co-ordination between the three services of several countries.

RIGHT
A woman factory worker handles strips of Window (also known as chaff), aluminium strips that reflected radar signals in order to confuse observers about the size and nature of a radar blip. The deception plan for the Normandy invasion, codenamed Operation *Fortitude*, made use of Window in order to confuse German radar into thinking that an invasion fleet was headed for the Pas de Calais. Such passive countermeasures had great effect considering their relatively cheap cost.

LEFT
US B-17 bombers attack a key communications centre on the continent. A crucial element in the build-up to D-Day was the bombing of bridges, roads and railways that were likely to be used in moving reinforcements to threatened Normandy. This resulted in a heavy level of civilian casualties and some disruption to traffic, but the most effective use of air power in Normandy was in close air support. A strafing run on 17 July by a fighter even wounded the German commander in Normandy, Field Marshal Rommel.

ABOVE
Gliders strewn about the Normandy farmland testify to the arrival of the British 6th Airborne Division in Normandy. The Allies deployed three airborne divisions in the attack, to seize strategic points inland of the beaches and to seal off parts of the invasion area from reinforcement.

RIGHT
Troops of the Canadian Régiment de la Chaudière come ashore at Juno beach aboard their landing craft. Specialist armour, known as the "Funnies" is visible in the background. These vehicles were adapted to perform engineering tasks, and their use on Omaha might have saved many American lives. The Americans, however, were sceptical about such devices.

RIGHT
One of the few Robert Capa photographs to survive the development process shows US troops sheltering behind obstacles on Omaha Beach. While the American assault to the west on Utah Beach, benefited from some good fortune, the attack on Omaha was the only one of the five Allied landings to come close to failure.

LEFT
US Army medics treat battlefield casualties on a Normandy beach. Medics had to make quick decisions on how to deal with the wounded given the scant resources available. They knew how to bandage wounds, transfuse blood and offer some pain relieving drugs. The main pain reliever was morphine, which soldiers might even use on a mortally wounded man, if only to keep him quiet to die in peace. The medic's sole items of self-defence were a dirty white armband and a dirty Red Cross painted on his helmet.

RIGHT
A US mortar crew ducks as the round is launched against German positions in Normandy. Every US infantry company of four platoons included a small mortar battery to provide close fire support at hand. The effectiveness of mortar rounds on morale was considerable, in spite of their small calibre, as they arrived with less noise – and therefore less warning.

ABOVE
US soldiers fighting through Normandy hedgerows. While the British became bogged down in a fierce battle against the main body of German tanks in the west, the Americans were instead slowed by the terrain. Each field in Normandy was a potential small fortress thanks to the earthen banks topped by twisted, tightly woven hedges, characteristic of the farmland. In the end, the invention of the equivalent of a large garden fork, welded to the front of tanks, provided the solution – to rip holes in the hedgerows.

ABOVE
General Charles de Gaulle, who had kept a "Fighting France" in the war, walks down the Champs Elysées on 26 August 1944. De Gaulle had refused to surrender with the rest of the French army in June 1940, and was regarded by Vichy France as a traitor. Nor did his British and American Allies seem altogether comfortable dealing with this haughty man. But his belief in his cause and his determination to be treated with due respect as the leader of his nation's resistance are worthy of the highest respect.

REVENGE WEAPONS

In October 1939, a letter was passed to the British Embassy in Oslo, Norway. Inside were a proximity fuse and a long report detailing some of the key weapons programmes being worked on by the German arms industry. One involved rocket-propelled weapons. This was the first warning the British received of the biggest German technological advance of the war. Attacks began on southern England using these rocket weapons on 12 June 1944. On 8 September, a huge explosion in London heralded the arrival of a new weapon, the rocket-powered V-2. (V in both cases stood for *Vergeltungswaffen*, or revenge weapons.) In the absence of an air force capable of strategic attacks, the Germans developed missile weapons that needed no pilot, merely a calculation of fuel and to be pointed in the right direction.

ABOVE
The V-1 was a pilotless aircraft. It could be shot down or, as in this case, flipped over by an aircraft's wing slid beneath one of its fins. The silence as the bomb fell to earth following the cutting-out of their engine was a moment of high stress for those in the targeted area.

RIGHT
The V-2, a forerunner of today's nuclear-tipped missiles, basically flew up and then silently fell back to earth, until the massive explosion marked its detonation. Unlike the V-1, there was no defence against a V-2, except the luck of not being in the wrong place at the wrong time.

ABOVE
A police officer offers sympathy to a South London resident whose house had been demolished by a V-1 attack one Sunday while he was out walking the dog. His wife perished in the explosions.

RIGHT

The Italian Fascist leader Mussolini views the wreckage of the conference room in Hitler's headquarters at Rastenburg, East Prussia, after the attempted assassination of the German dictator on 20 July 1944. The plot would have succeeded had an officer not unknowingly moved the bomb, contained in a briefcase. The conspirators were motivated by the recognition that the war was lost, and Germany ought to be spared further destruction.

BELOW

Workers assemble Lancasters in a British aircraft plant. The ultimate reason for Germany's defeat was the overwhelming of her economy by the far superior industrial capacity of the Allied nations.

THE PACIFIC WAR

After the battles of Midway and Guadalcanal in 1942, the outcome of the Pacific war was never in doubt. But that did not stop the Japanese making life very hard for the Allies. Attacks on the Japanese came on three fronts. The least threatening to them was from India, where a predominantly British and Indian army probed at the Japanese, until they responded with a counter-attack on India that ended in defeat at the twin battles of Imphal and Kohima in 1944. A second thrust, originating in Australia, pushed up the Solomon Islands chain, New Guinea and neighbouring islands, ultimately aiming at the Philippines. Finally, the US Navy supported a third axis of attack across the central Pacific, starting at Tarawa, which eventually reached the Marianas in 1944. The Japanese fought very hard against each of these attacks, but the far-flung nature of the fighting left most of their forces poorly supplied, severely hampering their combat effectiveness.

ABOVE
A US Navy corpsman administers a blood transfusion in the field to a wounded US Marine on the island of Saipan in June 1944. Saipan was identified as the location for an airbase for B-29 strategic bombers, then about to enter service. The B-29s had a very long range and would be able to bomb Japanese cities from a base here. Two Marine divisions landed on 15 June, and the battle ended on 9 July, when the Americans witnessed the astonishing sight of 8,000 Japanese civilians (out of some 20,000 on the island) hurling themselves off cliffs into shark-infested waters, rather than surrender.

7

LEFT
The pilot of a Grumman F6F climbs out of the cockpit after his plane crashed while trying to land on the USS *Yorktown*. The Japanese fleet attempted to intervene against its American counterpart off Saipan on 19 June. Some 400 aircraft were sent against the Americans, but US Navy F6Fs shot down 300 and drove the others off. The engagement became known as "the Great Marianas Turkey Shoot".

ABOVE
The Japanese battleship *Musashi* evades attacking aircraft on 24 October 1944 during the battle of the Sibuyan Sea. This combat was part of four separate engagements over two days known as the battle of Leyte Gulf, considered the largest naval battle in history. The Japanese attempted to defeat the American invasion force attacking the Philippines island of Leyte, but were themselves beaten in each of the three engagements. The fate of the *Musashi* demonstrated how the era of the battleship was at an end – the aircraft struck her with bombs and torpedoes, sinking her.

ABOVE
General Douglas MacArthur returns to the Philippines on 20 October 1944. The Japanese had subjected the American army in the Philippines to a humiliating defeat in 1942 and MacArthur had fled, leaving his troops behind to endure a Japanese prison. Many died, but MacArthur made a promise to return with an army and took great pride in fulfilling his word. The liberation of the Philippines was completed in early 1945.

THE END OF GERMANY

With the liberation of Paris on 25 August 1944, the German withdrawal verged on a rout. On the Eastern Front, a massive Red Army offensive in Belorussia launched on 22 June 1944, the third anniversary of the invasion of Russia, obliterated an entire German army group in the course of a month's fighting. For the Allies the fighting got tougher on both fronts as they neared the German borders and supply lines became stretched. In the west, an attempt to take a crossing over the Rhine at Arnhem in September 1944 ended in failure, and a dreadful battle in the Hürtgen Forest, now largely forgotten, but at the time a byword for horror among American soldiers, began in the same month. The Germans were presented with a pause that allowed them to launch an offensive in December 1944 in the Ardennes, known as the battle of the Bulge. This ended in a crushing defeat. Attacked from east and west once the spring thaw began, Germany was doomed. Hitler shot himself on 30 April 1945 as the Red Army battled its way into Berlin and the Germans surrendered on 7 May 1945.

ABOVE
British paratroops land at a dropping zone to the west of the town of Arnhem. The attack on Arnhem was planned by Montgomery and was the largest airborne operation in history. Several major river crossings needed to be seized, while a British armoured spearhead surged up a narrow road to reach the bridge at Arnhem. But the plan relied on too many things going perfectly, when war is all about coping with plans going wrong either through bad luck or enemy intervention, and the blame for its failure lies with Montgomery.

ABOVE
Members of the 1st SS Panzer Division check road signs during their advance in the early part of the Battle of the Bulge. Hitler's offensive benefited in its first days from poor flying weather, which hindered Allied air operations. The initial attacks resulted in some of the worst moments in American military history: the 106th Infantry Division was routed, with 8,000 of its soldiers surrendering to the Germans. Malmédy, a town whose name appears on one of the signposts, was the scene of one of the worst atrocities committed by the Germans against American soldiers, when 84 were murdered by SS troops. The offensive ended in failure, however, as American reinforcements stiffened the front, and the weather cleared.

ABOVE
Soldiers of the US 82nd Airborne Division march through the snow during the American counterattack on the Bulge salient. The aftermath of the Bulge is often overlooked by short histories of the war, but it was a difficult fight. The highest single month total for American casualties during the campaign in northwestern Europe came at exactly this point, January 1945.

ABOVE
American armoured troops guard the Ludendorff railroad bridge at Remagen in March 1945. The bridge was supposed to have been demolished by German engineers, but remained standing after the charges failed to destroy it effectively. This gave the Allies one crossing across the river Rhine for ten days, long enough to secure a bridgehead on the other side, and construct a pontoon bridge to substitute for the Remagen bridge.

ABOVE
American and Red Army troops share a joke on the Elbe river in April 1945. Hitler had hoped that the two armies, rivals in ideology, would start shooting at one another before they had finished shooting at the German soldiers. However, the alliance held until Germany had been conquered and for a few years thereafter. But leaders on both sides were already preparing for future hostility between them.

LEFT
A sergeant of the reconnaissance troop of the 1st Battalion, 756th Rifle Regiment of the Red Army hoists the victory banner over the Reichstag in Berlin at 2.25 pm on 30 April 1945. Although German troops still occupied the building, the whole structure was in Soviet hands by 11 pm. The war was not quite over, but the massive Soviet offensive launched on 16 April had secured the German capital.

ABOVE
Corpses of victims of a concentration camp lie in serried ranks as American soldiers view the Nazis' darkest secret. The machinery of the death camps was set in motion in January 1942, after a conference of middle level Nazi officials at Wannsee. The conference was conducted on the orders of Hermann Göring, and in effect industrialized the murder of European Jews.

ABOVE
German civilians forced into visiting death camps, on the order of General Dwight Eisenhower, the Allies' supreme commander. Most Germans who could plausibly deny all knowledge of the murder of the Jews did so, although those living near the camps must have been aware of trains entering and leaving at a steady rate.

FINISHING OFF JAPAN

After the Marianas had been occupied by America in mid-1944, and the attack on the Philippines had begun, the Americans planned the invasion of Japan. The first prerequisite was to acquire bases closer to the Japanese home islands. The island of Iwo Jima was selected for the first attack, in early 1945, and the second target was the island of Okinawa, a part of Japan proper. The Japanese prepared special squadrons of suicide pilots known as *kamikaze* (meaning "divine wind", a reference to a storm that had destroyed a Mongol invasion fleet in the thirteenth century) to attack warships. But even such self-immolation could not thwart the American plans. The British unleashed their own offensive in Burma, while the Red Army was about to attack in Manchuria in August 1945, when the United States dropped the first atomic bomb on Hiroshima.

ABOVE
The USS *Franklin* lists heavily to starboard after being struck by kamikaze aircraft during operations. In spite of the serious damage, the *Franklin* managed to return to Brooklyn Navy Yard on the Atlantic coast of North America, thanks to the American navy's careful attention to damage control.

RIGHT
American marines hoist the flag over Mount Suribachi on Iwo Jima on 23 February 1945, in this Joseph Rosenthal photograph. It was the second flag raised there, replacing one on a smaller flag pole. More US Marine Medals of Honor were won on Iwo Jima than in any other battle in American history. Nearly 7,000 American soldiers were killed, and 22,000 Japanese.

391
807 807
USMC

LEFT
War matériel is unloaded from LSTs (Landing Ships, Tank) on Iwo Jima. A huge armada kept American forces (on land, sea and air) supplied on their drive across the Pacific, and the sheer scale of it dwarfed Japanese expectations of what the American war effort could support.

LEFT
The characteristic mushroom cloud of an atomic bomb looms over the city of Hiroshima on 6 August 1945. The Second World War was the only nuclear war so far in history, and arguments continue over whether the bombing was necessary, or whether it was much of a threat against Stalin as an attempt to force Japan's surrender.

ABOVE
General Douglas MacArthur, the Allied supreme commander in Japan, signs the instrument of surrender aboard the USS *Missouri* in Tokyo Bay on 2 September 1945. The Second World War had ended, six years after it had begun.

THE END OF EMPIRES

1945–1999

At the end of the Second World War, both Britain and France had used up most of their national wealth in fighting for national survival and were heavily in debt. The United States, although supportive of the two countries in their war against Germany, had traditionally not been particularly enthusiastic about helping them to maintain their empires. The mood of the times was also no longer imperialistic, and the citizens of Britain and France had more important worries than fighting wars to maintain their colonial possessions, which frequently cost more to own than they repaid.

In 1947, India was granted independence by Britain, and divided into two states. Having lost the most important part of its empire, the rest of the British possessions also gradually gained independence, although not without some conflicts. France was slower to reliquish its empire, but both these grand projects had more or less ceased to exist by 1965. Nasty wars occurred in places where there had been substantial settlement from the imperial powers, such as Kenya and Algeria. The worst conflict occurred in Vietnam, where France, with heavy support from the United States, fought a war that was both a traditional colonial war against natives opposing foreign rule and also a part of the growing conflict between capitalist states, led by the United States, and the supposed menace of international communism led by the Soviet Union.

The conflicts created a new military term "counter-insurgency warfare", and provided many parallels both attended to and ignored during the Vietnam War.

LEFT
Viet Minh fighters take up ambush positions along a river in Vietnam.

THE FRENCH INDOCHINA WAR 1946–1954

The colonial authorities in French Indochina had been associated with the discredited Vichy regime, and with defeated Japan. A communist-inspired nationalist movement, the Viet Minh, proclaimed independence in the north, while the French, with British and American backing, sought to re-impose their rule. War broke out in December and a guerrilla conflict ensued. Successes in September 1950, led to a more general Viet Minh offensive in early 1951. The move was premature, and the Viet Minh were defeated. In 1953 the Viet Minh attacked into Laos, the French countered by occupying Dien Bien Phu, which became the setting for a great Viet Minh victory in 1954, after which the French abandoned Indochina.

LEFT
Two French soldiers capture a Viet Minh soldier. The French army lacked the numbers and support in the important Red River region, in the north of the country, to wage a successful campaign there.

RIGHT
Foreign Legion paratroops land at Dien Bien Phu. The French hoped that they could establish a base here that could be used to send columns of troops to attack the Viet Minh's own bases in north-western Vietnam. They would rely on aircraft to supply the base, and on their artillery to defend it.

ABOVE
Viet Minh troops attack a French strongpoint during the battle of Dien Bien Phu. The French army had gambled that the Viet Minh would be unable to assemble a strong enough army to capture the base. However, the Viet Minh put great effort into constructing a supply network to lay siege to it. Once the Viet Minh positioned their own artillery and anti-aircraft guns around Dien Bien Phu, the French scheme was doomed. The base finally fell on 7 May 1954.

THE END OF THE BRITISH EMPIRE, 1948–1964

Nationalist movements arose in many parts of the British Empire during the first half of the twentieth century. The immense cost of the Second World War and the economic crises that followed victory in 1945 left Britain with little option but to reduce its imperial possessions abroad, simply because it was becoming too expensive to maintain the military presence needed there. Once India had been granted independence in 1947, it was only a matter of time before the rest of the empire began to slip from Britain's grasp, as much of it had been acquired to protect communications with the subcontinent. However, in some countries, nationalist guerrilla movements attempted to accelerate that process. Key struggles were waged in Malaya (perhaps the only genuinely profitable colony), Kenya (where a small but significant group of white settlers complicated matters) and Rhodesia (where a larger group of white settlers attempted to maintain the old ways). Important lessons about counter-insurgency warfare were learnt in each of these conflicts.

ABOVE
Men of the élite Special Air Service (SAS) Regiment of the British Army on patrol in the Malayan jungle. The insurgents during the Malayan Emergency, which began in 1948, were predominantly ethnic Chinese. This was their weakness, as they had little support among the majority Malay population. The British found that a system of resettlement and economic development, combined with aggressive patrolling in guerrilla base areas and a promise of eventual independence, maintained their influence and removed most of the reasons to support the insurgency. Malaya became independent in 1957, and the Emergency ended in 1960.

LEFT
A British soldier stands guard over suspected insurgents during the Mau Mau uprising in Kenya in 1953. The revolt in Kenya resulted from unwillingness on the part of a small community of some 30,000 white settlers to surrender any of their political or economic power in the country. The result was an insurgency that began in January 1953. The British countered with harsh policies: rounding up likely leaders, interning suspects into camps, and aggressive patrolling through Mau Mau operational areas. The Mau Mau were defeated militarily, but, as in Malaya, the British also conceded several key political reforms, which restricted the pool of potential rebels by giving some a stake in the colony's economy.

ALGERIAN WAR OF INDEPENDENCE, 1954–1962

France had incorporated its Algerian colonists as a self-governing department following the Revolution of 1848. However, the majority Muslim Algerian population was largely excluded from the political administration of the country. Following the Viet Minh success in Indochina, the Algerians launched their own war for independence in November 1954. The war was one of almost outright terrorism. Algerian nationalists did develop an army of trained and disciplined soldiers, mostly deployed just across the border in neighbouring Tunisia and Morocco. There were also political gestures, such as the general strike in Algiers in 1957. But for the most part the war was one of hit-and-run raids, bombings, ambushes, murders and torture, means used by both sides. While the French military had more or less won the conflict by 1959, having rendered the nationalists' military forces within Algeria almost ineffective, the political battle for the hearts and minds of the French people was being lost. In 1959, following a change of regime, President Charles de Gaulle suggested "self-determination" as the solution. A period of political turmoil ended in an agreement to grant independence to Algeria and, on 3 July 1962, French rule over the North African country came to an end.

RIGHT
Paratroops restrain a crowd of French colonists in Algeria in April 1961. Following de Gaulle's apparent abandonment of the cause of a French Algeria, there were two attempts among the colonists to conduct an insurrection of their own to bring about the fall of the president, who had only come to power with the army's support in 1958. In January 1960, the French colonists in Algeria launched a popular rising that failed when the bulk of the army stood by the regime. In April 1961, it was the generals' turn, but their insurrection was limited to Algeria, while the army and air force of metropolitan France stood by de Gaulle.

025162

ABOVE
Algerian exiles stand at the Morice Line, a fence of barbed wire and electrified wire that extended hundreds of miles along the Algerian-Tunisian border. The fence proved remarkably successful, as attempts to break the electrified portions were signalled to monitoring stations, allowing the French military to send troops rapidly to hunt down anyone crossing illegally. Few Algerian guerrillas successfully breached the line.

ABOVE
An Indian army machine-gun team takes up position to give cover to advancing troops on the Lahore front in the 1965 war. Both the Indian and Pakistani armies initially drew on their British military heritage for their armies, although over time they developed more distinctive personalities.

THE INDO–PAKISTANI WARS 1947–1999

In 1947, India was partitioned between predominantly Muslim areas and Hindu-majority regions. The result was a substantial resettlement of people, during which many were brutally murdered, a result of centuries of sectarian distrust. In Kashmir, where northern India and West Pakistan met, a Hindu monarch ruled over a Muslim population. Pakistani tribesmen attempted to take over Kashmir in October 1947, and the monarch fled to India, where in return for Indian support, he was forced to agree to allow India to annex Kashmir. When spring came, a full-scale war in Kashmir broke out between India and Pakistan, and Kashmir ended up partitioned between the two. Three further wars ensued, growing out of the rivalries established in the 1947 war. In 1965, six weeks of fighting ended in another stalemate. In 1971, Bangladesh (formerly East Pakistan) gained its independence with Indian help. A final round in the conflict occurred in 1999, back in Kashmir, with the outbreak of the Kargil War.

RIGHT
Pakistani troops on the East Pakistani border in November 1971 watch for the impending Indian invasion. India attacked on 4 December. The crisis in East Pakistan gave India a justification to go to war with Pakistan for the third time in 25 years. The overwhelming victory in the east was not matched by similar success in the west, where neither side secured a major advantage.

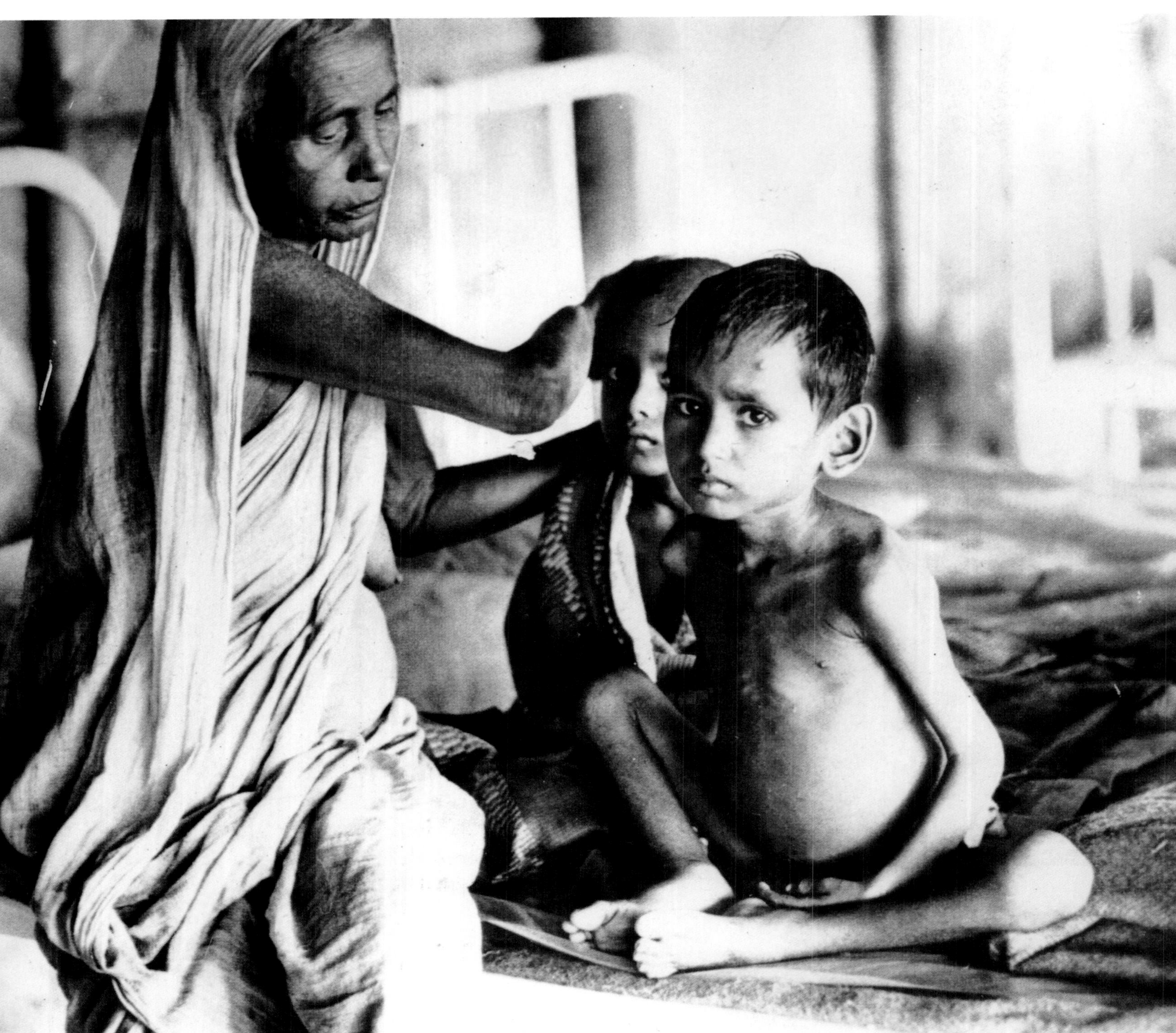

ABOVE
A Bangladeshi woman comforts her grandchildren in a Calcutta hospital in 1971. The 1971 war broke out after a long civil conflict in East Pakistan. An East Pakistani party won a majority of seats in the 1970 election for Pakistan's parliament, but it was not allowed to form a government by West Pakistani politicians and the army. A repressive martial law regime was imposed on East Pakistan, and millions of refugees fled to India.

ABOVE
Bangladeshis celebrate the India victory in the 1971 war. An East Pakistani resistance movement, the Mukti Bahini, was formed after the rejection of the 1970 election results. Its brutal suppression created the crisis that led to war.

ABOVE

Pakistani gunners prepare to fire a 105mm pack Howitzer during the Kargil conflict in 1999. The conflict arose from the unsettled situation of Kashmir. Pakistan sponsored Azad Kashmiri (Free Kashmir) insurgents who regularly crossed the border to attack Indian army outposts near the Line of Control, the effective border between Pakistani- and Indian-controlled Kashmir.

THE ZIMBABWE INDEPENDENCE WAR

The last major military action in the process of decolonization came in Zimbabwe (previously Southern Rhodesia). In 1964, the white minority population declared unilateral independence for Rhodesia, rather than bow to the British government's preference for an orderly transition to black-majority rule. Black African nationalists formed a guerrilla resistance movement that struggled for some years without any great success, but which gradually eroded Rhodesian resources. Rhodesia was heavily dependent on South African economic and military support, and on the continued existence of a Portuguese African empire embracing the colonies of Mozambique and Angola. Once Mozambique and Angola became independent in 1975, the war widened disastrously for Rhodesian whites as the anti-government guerrillas were able to operate from bases in Mozambique. South Africa soon decided that Rhodesia governed by whites was unsustainable in the long run, and negotiations resulted in a return of Rhodesia to British rule in 1979, and subsequent independence as Zimbabwe in 1980. The great European colonial empires had now all but vanished.

RIGHT
Rhodesian soldiers track guerrillas during the 1970s. The Rhodesian army developed some exceptionally successful counter-insurgency techniques using whatever equipment they could acquire on the weapons black market.

安永齒科醫院

THE COLD WARS

1947–1989

In 1947 the United States announced that it would take over the support of the Greek government in conducting its war with communist guerrilla forces for control of the country. From this point, the United States formally committed itself to contesting through aid or force, any political movement that appeared to be subject to strong Soviet influence. The Soviet Union and the United States had regarded one another with some suspicion even when allied against Nazi Germany during the Second World War. Having become the world's two greatest powers in the course of that conflict, their future rivalry was only to be expected.

Several wars grew out of this competition. The conflict in Korea was the most intense of them, with the war being launched with the blessing of the Soviet dictator, Joseph Stalin. The United Nations sent a largely American army to resist a North Korean attack on the south, which it was able to do thanks in part to the Soviet boycott of United Nations Security Council meetings: the Soviets were therefore unable to exercise their veto against such intervention. But the conflict was largely waged in the shadowy world of espionage, and in a technological race to develop weapons systems, especially methods of delivering a nuclear device.

The Cold War was also fought through the media. Both the Soviet Union and the United States funded print and other media in a long-running propaganda campaign. As such, war photography became for both sides another tool in the conflict.

LEFT
South Korean troops, armed with US M1 carbines, check buildings for snipers.

LEFT

A North Korean T-34 tank under air attack. The T-34 gave the North Koreans a significant advantage in their initial attack, as neither US nor South Korean forces had enough weapons sufficiently powerful to penetrate its thick armour.

KOREA

In August 1945, the United States and the Soviet Union agreed to divide the Korean peninsula into two occupation zones, with the dividing line being the 38th parallel. In June 1950, the North Koreans, supported by the Soviet Union, launched an invasion of South Korea to unify the country by force. Although the North Koreans secured control of much of the country, US aid enabled the South Koreans to hold on to the port of Pusan, in the south-east of the country. A large US force, organized under the authority of the United Nations, then struck at Inchon. The result was a North Korean withdrawal to the Chinese border by November 1950. The Chinese then intervened. They surprised the United Nations forces and drove them southward again. The front line eventually stabilized in May 1951, roughly in the vicinity of the 38th parallel. Two years of grim fighting ensued, reminiscent of the First World War. A truce was agreed in July 1953. No peace treaty has yet formally ended the war.

RIGHT
US Marines approach Inchon in a landing craft. The idea of striking at Inchon, near Seoul, and far to the rear of the main fighting around Pusan, was General Douglas MacArthur's. It enabled him to cut the supply lines of the North Korean forces, and threaten their political regime in the north.

BELOW
American troops scale the sea wall at Inchon. The operation presented considerable difficulties, because the tidal range at Inchon is one of the highest in the world. The North Koreans did not have strong forces in the area, and the landing forces were able to move on Seoul, although the fighting there dragged on for almost ten days.

ABOVE
US soldiers engage snipers during street-fighting in a Korean town. The war caused serious damage to towns and cities as fighting passed through them, destroying the locality in order to liberate it.

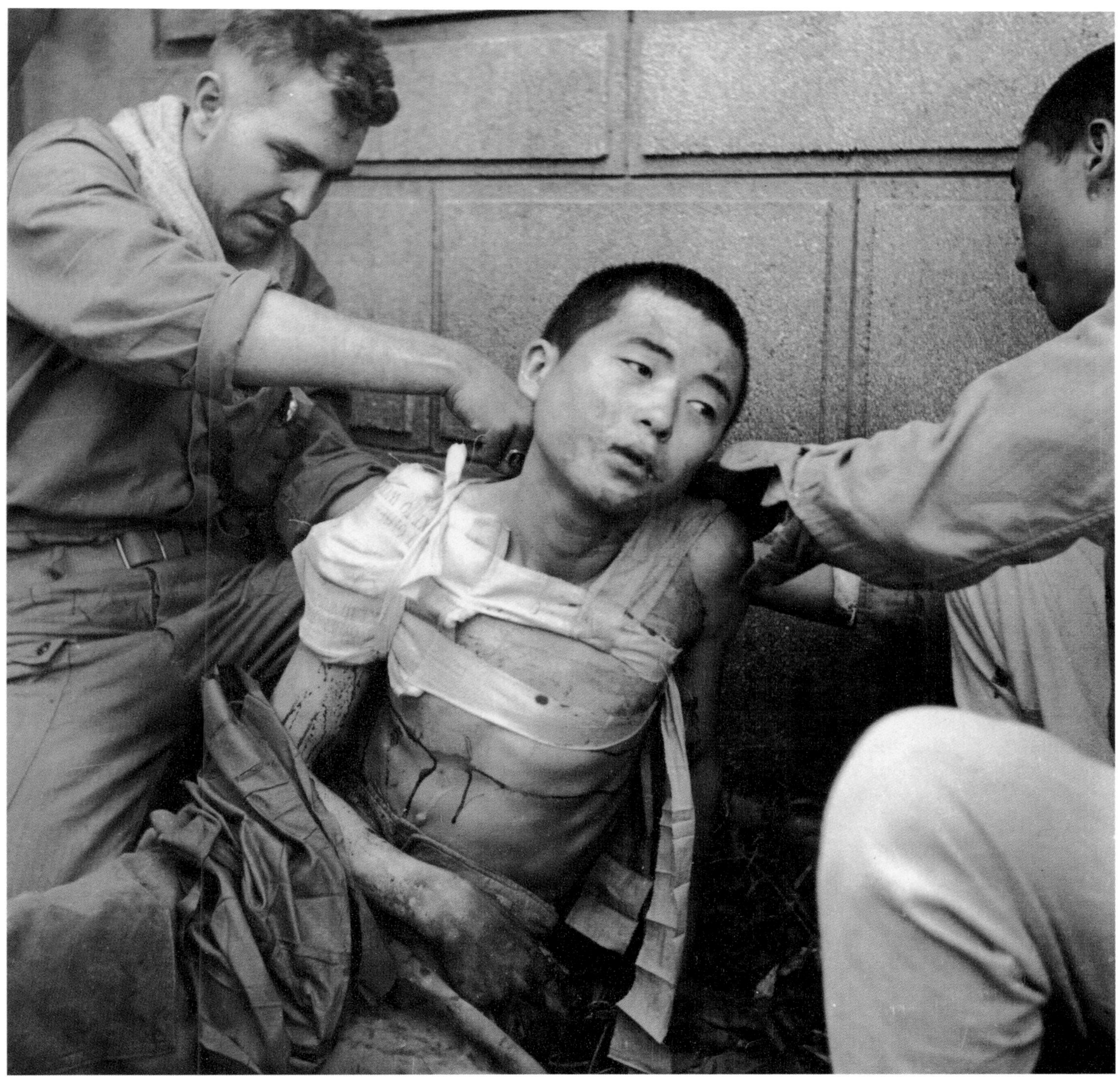

ABOVE
Medics help a boy injured in the Inchon invasion. A heavy bombardment preceded the landings, and the direct assault on Seoul led to high losses among civilians. Enveloping Seoul and taking more time over the attack might have saved many civilian lives, but MacArthur was in a hurry.

ABOVE
Two US soldiers find a game of warfare offers some relief from the boredom of non-combat army life. The Korean War itself turned into a deadly chess game once the mobile phase ended, as each side manoeuvred to gain small advantages on the front-line.

BELOW

A burial ceremony inters another casualty of the war. The scale of the Korean War has been largely forgotten. Over a million Americans served in the war, and double that number of Chinese, plus further combatants from, among others, the Soviet Union, Britain, Canada, Australia, New Zealand, Belgium, France, Greece, the Netherlands, the Philippines, Thailand, Turkey, Colombia and Ethiopia.

THE CUBAN REVOLUTION 1958–1959

Cuba's politics had been marred by more than 25 years of dictatorship and corrupt elections when, in 1956, an 80-strong group determined to start an armed resistance, landed in the Oriente province. Although most were killed or captured in the first battle, a dozen, including their leader, Fidel Castro, escaped and began recruiting a guerrilla army. After two years of recruitment, Castro launched an attack towards the west of the island, in two columns. The regime of Cuban dictator Fulgencio Batista was incompetently administered and corrupt. Its inefficient police and armed forces proved no match for the rebels in a fair fight, and on 1 January 1959 Batista fled as his army virtually melted away. The relative ease of the victory gave a fillip to the idea that guerrilla warfare can be decisive. The circumstances of Cuba in 1958 were vital to Castro's success, a lesson that his associate, Che Guevara, did not properly comprehend. Guevara perished in 1967, attempting to duplicate the Cuban victory in Bolivia.

ABOVE LEFT
Rifles held aloft, Castro's soldiers celebrate their triumph outside the presidential palace in Havana. Castro's revolution at first seemed propelled more by a sense of injustice than by ideology. However, ideology became increasingly significant after Castro's attempt at agrarian reform valued land taken from American-based companies at the value assessed for tax purposes rather than its true market value. As the support of the United States cooled, Castro turned to the Soviet Union for help, especially for the supply of oil. Eventually, a peculiarly intense Cold War between the United States and Cuba broke out, which continued throughout Castro's life.

ABOVE
Anti-Castro exiles captured during the Bay of Pigs landings in April 1961. These were organized and funded by the United States. The tensions created by this operation contributed to the arrival of Soviet nuclear weapons in Cuba in the autumn of 1962, and the consequent missile crisis in October.

SPHERES OF INFLUENCE

The Cold War was marked by the division of the world into spheres of Soviet and American influence. Much attention in the West has focused on Soviet policing of their own sphere in Eastern Europe. But the United States, too, kept its own "backyard" under a watchful eye. Guatemala in 1954, the Dominican Republic in 1965 and Chile in 1973, were all occasions when governments considered vulnerable to Soviet influence were overthrown by the US. The Americans also influenced political affairs of more distant countries, eyeing the communist movements in France and Italy with concern, and in the latter case refusing to countenance communist participation in government in the 1970s. However, the acceptance of spheres of influence produced stability in a tense situation. The Cuban Missile Crisis both brought the world the closest it has yet come to nuclear war, and also marked the beginning of the gradual thawing of the Cold War.

BELOW LEFT

This classic photograph by Josef Koudelka, shows a Czech protesting against Soviet tanks rolling down the streets of Prague in 1968. The Soviet Union guarded the latitude allowed to communist regimes of Eastern Europe carefully. In the case of Hungary in 1956 and Czechoslovakia in 1968, their Communist governments went too far in liberating the regimes and it required a heavy-handed intervention to bring them into line.

BELOW

A Chilean soldier guards prisoners kept in the national stadium after the 11 September 1973 coup that overthrew Salvador Allende's government. The Americans saw democratically elected leftist regimes in Latin America as threats. In the case of Chile, no expense was spared in subverting Allende's administration. When this did not work, the Americans paid the army to take care of it. A brutal repression that cost 4,000 lives followed.

VIETNAM

1962–1975

The United States established a formal military presence in Vietnam as early as 1950, when the Military Assistance and Advisory Group, Indochina, was formed. However, serious escalation of the US military presence only began under the administration of President John F. Kennedy, who in December 1961 announced that the number of American advisors would be increased from under a thousand to 3,200. The Military Assistance Command, Vietnam was founded in February 1962, and perhaps marks the moment when US leaders decided that the conflict in Vietnam was worth risking their nation's prestige for.

The escalation proceeded only gradually. Advisors were not meant to take on combat roles, although they frequently did. As the situation of the pro-American regime in the South Vietnamese capital of Saigon grew more precarious, the Americans introduced more aid. In August 1964, an incident between US Navy destroyers and North Vietnamese vessels was deemed to be an attack. An undeclared war by the United States against North Vietnam was then formally launched with the passing of the Tonkin Gulf Resolution. The war properly opened in March 1965 with the beginning of a campaign of bombing raids and the deployment of American combat troops.

The full panoply of the United States' armed forces was deployed against the North Vietnamese in the ensuing eight years. Strategic bombers, helicopters, battleships, tanks and troops all saw action. The war was also used as a test ground for a variety of academic approaches to quantifying the effects of weapons. Scientific solutions, such as the use of defoliants to reduce the cover provided by thick vegetation, were adopted to solve specific operational problems faced by the Americans and their allies.

LEFT
South Vietnamese troops move past a hut they have set afire after finding Viet Cong propaganda leaflets inside.

THE ERA OF "MILITARY ADVISORS"

After the Geneva Accords of July 1954 were agreed, leaving Vietnam a divided country, the US Military Assistance and Advisory Group, Indochina, became the US Military Assistance and Advisory Group, Vietnam. American forces played a limited role initially, as the South Vietnamese army was small, and organized opposition to the American-sponsored government in Saigon was slight. However, after the South Vietnamese failed to conduct elections in accordance with the Geneva agreement, the North Vietnamese began to organize armed resistance with the intent of unifying the two Vietnams by force. The numbers of American soldiers deployed to Vietnam steadily increased, and by the end of 1962 there were 16,000 there. At the beginning of 1963, a South Vietnamese army operation with heavy American support was conducted at Ap Bac. It was a significant failure and American military leaders in Washington began increasingly to regard the deployment of US combat troops as the only practical solution to winning the war.

ABOVE
An H-21 helicopter of the US Army hovers above soldiers during the fighting in 1962. The helicopter is the weapons system most closely identified with the Vietnam War. American pilots flew helicopters such as this to ferry South Vietnamese troops into action, and also as gunships on fire support missions.

ABOVE
North Vietnamese soldiers train South Vietnamese volunteers to fight as guerrillas against the South Vietnamese government and the Americans. In 1962, the Americans introduced a system of "protected hamlets" that forced people from their original homes into defended areas in an attempt to control the guerrillas' access to potential supporters. In fact, the system led to more recruits for the Viet Cong (the North-Vietnamese-sponsored guerrilla movement), driven by resentment at being driven from their homes.

ABOVE
A South Vietnamese soldier helps a comrade out of the mud in the Mekong Delta in 1962. The South Vietnamese army at this time was well equipped, but its officers were more concerned with their relationship to the government of the country, a paranoid, authoritarian regime led by Ngo Dinh Diem, than in fighting the Viet Cong.

AMERICAN TROOPS INTO COMBAT

In November 1963, the corrupt Diem government was overthrown, and Diem assassinated, in a coup in which his former American sponsors played a key role. The Kennedy administration had concluded that it was hopeless to prop up Diem's regime any longer. Kennedy himself was making increasingly ambiguous statements about the war and seemed to be positioning himself to be able either to withdraw American military support or to escalate it dramatically. His own assassination three weeks later placed his Vice President, Lyndon Johnson, in charge of American policy. Johnson had been an advocate of "winning the war" at a key August 1963 meeting. After weighing up the advice he received and following the Tonkin Gulf Incident, when a US destroyer claimed to be under attack by North Vietnamese torpedo boats, Johnson sent American combat troops to Vietnam and threw the full weight of the American military against the Viet Cong. The result was a strategy of attrition, as the US Army attempted to find and destroy the Viet Cong, while the US Air Force bombed strategic targets in North Vietnam.

ABOVE

US Marines go ashore during an operation in the Mekong Delta in 1965. The "search and destroy" strategy of the Americans relied on using their considerable superiority in firepower against the Viet Cong. However well meaning on arrival, the American soldier found himself in a foreign country, fighting among people who spoke the language of the enemy, and whose own thoughts and feelings about the American presence were likely to be mixed. It was a recipe for the type of misunderstandings that in war can lead to fatal errors.

ABOVE
During night-time operations, a Minigun fires from an AC-47 gunship. The conversion of Second World War era two-engined transports into fire-support aircraft incorporated three of these Miniguns. The Miniguns used prodigious amounts of ammunition. Able to fire 6,000 rounds a minute, they normally shot off between 300 and 700 rounds in a burst of fire lasting three to seven seconds. This was equivalent to the rate of fire per minute of Second World War era machine guns.

BELOW
A US Air Force F-4C Phantom jet looses off a barrage of rockets on a suspected Viet Cong village in the Mekong Delta. The American tactic was to use their immense superiority in firepower from artillery and aircraft to defeat the Viet Cong by killing large numbers of them. The main role of the infantry was to fix the Viet Cong position and call in fire support. It does not take much imagination to realize that many civilians found themselves at risk in such circumstances.

LEFT
US Air Force F-100 fighters launch air-to-ground missiles against targets in Vietnam. Rolling Thunder was the code name for an operation of continuous air bombardment of North Vietnam, which began 1965. The objective was to choke off the Viet Cong's supply line from the north via the Ho Chi Minh trail that ran through Laos and Cambodia. The trail itself was bombed, as were known concentrations of supplies and eventually even strategic installations around Hanoi.

LEFT
US infantry of the 173rd Airborne Brigade under Vietnamese fire during the battle for Dak To in November 1967. Dak To was a major confrontation between the US and North Vietnamese armies, and saw a considerable arsenal of technology deployed by the US forces, including chemical defoliants to clear forest areas in order to establish artillery fire bases, and "people sniffer" sensors that detected large concentrations of urine.

ABOVE
An official US Army photo shows part of a platoon of American infantry advancing through rice paddies during a clearing operation. Such operations involved extensive patrolling in order to drive Viet Cong forces out of populated areas. American official policy was to show great respect for private property, so as to encourage Vietnamese civilians to support the Saigon government.

RIGHT
Two marines help a wounded buddy to a helicopter landing zone where he could be evacuated for further medical treatment during Operation Prairie in Quang Tri in August–September 1966. The battles of Prairie were waged against North Vietnamese regular soldiers. The NVA (North Vietnamese Army) had moved units into South Vietnam toward the end of 1964, even before Johnson deployed American combat troops.

THE TET OFFENSIVE, 1968

After two-and-a-half years of search-and-destroy operations, including several major confrontations with North Vietnamese Army regulars, American military leaders privately admitted the war was deadlocked. They had placed their faith in statistical measures, believing the war was being waged scientifically, but the science was not working. The war was turning into another Verdun. The North Vietnamese, however, had a different idea. In the second half of 1967 they began to prepare for a major offensive in the south. First they launched several attacks near the demilitarized zone and in the Central Highlands, intending to draw in US troops. Then, on Tet, the day of the Lunar New Year (31 January 1968), they struck across Vietnam. The US armed forces restored the deadlock after heavy fighting, but Tet was still a strategic Vietnamese victory. Anti-war sentiment had been growing in the US, and Tet gave the lie to the positive public face being put on the American intervention, that it was a war being won.

LEFT

Field-standard hygiene (i.e. not much) and lack of sleep mark the face of a tired Marine, after a long patrol along the demilitarized zone separating North and South Vietnam. The Marines experienced heavy casualty rates, a reflection of their officers' aggressive approach to combat.

ABOVE

South Vietnamese soldiers fire their machine gun from a roof-top position during the fighting in Saigon. North Vietnamese commandos attacked a number of key strategic targets, including the US embassy, the presidential palace, and the main radio station. Accounts of the fierce street fighting which resulted were broadcast into American living rooms on the evening news.

ABOVE
One of the most important photographs of war ever taken (by Eddie Adams) shows the commander of the South Vietnamese police, General Nguyen Ngoc Loan, shooting a suspected Viet Cong. The incident was also captured on television film and shown on the NBC evening news. The general had previously made a name for himself brutally suppressing the opponents of Diem. The image of his apparent kangaroo court shocked Americans, and called into question the nature of the regime for which they were sending their young men to fight.

ABOVE
Camouflaged US Marines patrol the Demilitarized Zone in the aftermath of the Tet offensive. These are men of a Long Range Reconnaissance Patrol, a type of unit used to penetrate deep into the countryside around American bases for extended periods, relying on field craft, speed and silence instead of firepower when engaged by the enemy.

THE UNITED STATES TAKE A BACK SEAT

The Tet offensive mortally wounded the Johnson administration and its "search-and-destroy-plus-bombing strategy". Johnson abandoned plans to run for a second term, and in November 1968 Richard Nixon won the election for presidency. Nixon chose a characteristically devious strategy to engineer an end to American intervention. The Vietnamese would be put in the forefront of the fighting, which, given the poor state of their army, was tantamount to saying the war on the ground was lost. The bombing, however, would continue. Yet Nixon tried very hard to secure improved relations with the Soviet Union and with China and in doing so to use the leverage he gained to get those countries to put pressure on North Vietnam to negotiate an end to the war. So, while Nixon pursued his diplomatic strategy, the war on the ground continued. After some further fruitless search-and-destroy operations, such as the notorious battle of "Hamburger Hill" in the A Shau valley in May 1969, American troops played a less prominent role, but the bombing continued and, indeed, would escalate.

ABOVE
Green Beret infantry engage Vietnamese attacking their base near Ben Het in 1969. The "Vietnamization" policy required the South Vietnamese to replace American troops in the forefront of the fighting. Ben Het was heralded as a success as the South Vietnamese defenders sustained a 55-day battle and defeated the North Vietnamese attackers.

RIGHT
A MiG-17 is hit on the wing during a dogfight with a US airplane in 1968. The air defences over North Vietnam became increasingly dense as the war went on and incorporated anti-aircraft guns, surface-to-air missiles and fighters.

THE CAMBODIAN INCURSION, 1970

The long war in Vietnam caused considerable unrest in neighbouring Cambodia, and in January 1970 a coup toppled the neutralist regime led by Prince Norodom Sihanouk, a move which condemned the country to a generation of civil war, mass murder and turmoil. The North Vietnamese Army had long used bases in Cambodia to support its actions around Saigon and for some months these had been the targets of bombing by American aircraft. The Nixon administration, to show support for General Lon Nol, the pro-Western successor to Sihanouk, prepared an attack against the bases. American combat troops played a key role in aggressive action for the first time in some months. The offensive achieved little of importance, effectively just adding the needs of the corrupt and incompetent Lon Nol regime to those of the corrupt and incompetent Saigon government as drains on American resources in both matériel and prestige.

ABOVE
US army intelligence officers examine captured documents in Cambodia. The Americans expected to find an elaborate headquarters at the bases in Cambodia, but instead found a scattering of empty huts, as the Viet Cong had plenty of warning that the attack was coming.

ABOVE
American students gather round the corpse of one of their four fellow students who was shot by Ohio National Guard troops during demonstrations at Kent State University in May 1970. The Cambodian operations unleashed a wave of protests across the United States as fears grew that the Nixon administration would seek a renewal of the war effort that had proved so fruitless during the Johnson years.

LEFT
An American soldier guides helicopters to a landing zone in Cambodia in June 1970. Coloured smoke was used to tell the pilots whether the zone was "hot" (under enemy fire) or not. Soldiers also learned a set of hand-and-arm signals to guide the helicopter pilots in.

AMERICA RETREATS

The Nixon administration's plans to secure peace talks proved successful, and the North Vietnamese met with American negotiator Henry Kissinger in February 1970. The final phase of the war now began. While the negotiations went on, the Vietnamese continued the war. South Vietnamese troops became the main focus for North Vietnamese and Viet Cong attacks, part of a strategy to drive a wedge between the Saigon and Washington governments. However, the Americans did not want to look as though they were abandoning an ally. Thus, the North Vietnamese demand for a new coalition government in Saigon, incorporating Viet Cong ministers, proved the main stumbling block. The Saigon government also faced a dilemma: the United States demanded that they prosecute the war more effectively, but that necessitated a level of American support which was now no longer assured over the long term.

ABOVE
An American soldier expresses his hopes during operations in Tay Ninh province in September 1971. The Nixon administration's withdrawal of troops, together with the increasingly apparent futility of the war, produced a collapse of discipline among American draftees, as tensions at home over civil rights and the war spread across the Pacific. Mutinous behaviour, such as "fragging" (wounding or killing officers), became increasingly common.

RIGHT
A convoy transports American and South Vietnamese troops during Operation Lam Son 719 in February 1971. The aim was to destroy North Vietnamese bases in Laos and show the effectiveness of Vietnamization. But, when casualties reached a certain number, a retreat was ordered which turned into a rout – the final nail in the coffin of Vietnamization.

THE EASTER OFFENSIVE 1972

The North Vietnamese recognized that the Saigon government was losing the support of the Americans. Yet there was absolutely no chance of winning the war in the short term. The main goal was now to secure as much territory as possible before any truce or peace agreement with the United States was signed. The North Vietnamese Army and their Viet Cong allies were still outclassed by the South in the amount of firepower that they could deliver in support of operations. However, this did not deter the offensive they launched on 30 March. This time, the focus of operations was in the northern provinces. The North Vietnamese won some significant victories, occupying several provincial capitals. Again, US air power shifted the battle in favour of the South Vietnamese. Nixon, determined to get some kind of settlement that gave the United States "peace with honor", responded to the offensive with increased bombing of the north. This sustained campaign, begun in the wake of the North Vietnamese spring 1972 offensive and which intensified that autumn, eventually bore fruit in a peace agreement signed in Paris in January 1973.

LEFT

South Vietnamese soldiers gather after being brought by helicopter to the combat zone at An Loc during the spring offensive in 1972. The South Vietnamese fought well around An Loc, but again relied heavily on US air support to defeat the North Vietnamese and Viet Cong. By now the South Vietnamese had a million men in their army, outnumbering their North Vietnamese and Viet Cong opponents. But the morale amongst the Saigon regime's troops was very much lower, and the Americans frequently rued the fact that the North Vietnamese were more willing to die for their cause than the troops allied to the United States.

ABOVE
In another of the defining images of the war, Kim Phuc is shown crying from pain and shock, as she runs along a road after a napalm attack by South Vietnamese aircraft on her village of Trang Bang in June 1972. The photographer, Nick Ut, won a Pulitzer Prize for the shot. Kim Phuc later moved to Canada.

ABOVE
An aviator rushes to his aircraft in April 1972 aboard the USS *Constellation* as part of the operations to counter the Vietnamese spring offensive. American aircraft carriers played a key role throughout the war, acting as moving airfields at sea, which allowed air support to shift between targets in North and South Vietnam simply by sailing to the appropriate area from which to fly strikes.

CAMBODIAN CIVIL WAR

The Khmer Rouge were a Cambodian counterpart to the Viet Cong. They had received considerable assistance from the North Vietnamese when the latter believed that Prince Sihanouk intended to abandon neutrality and join with the Americans. The removal of Sihanouk by his prime minister, Lon Nol, was partly a product of the Khmer Rouge attacks in 1969. Lon Nol was keener to fight, but lacked an army capable of sustaining operations against the Khmer Rouge, and he rapidly lost control of most of the country except the capital, Phnom Penh. The collapse of the South Vietnamese regime in 1975 coincided with the fall of Lon Nol's hapless government, as the Khmer Rouge launched an offensive that swept it away like a house of cards. The Khmer Rouge then instituted one of the nastiest episodes in post-war history, as they turned their "revolution" into an excuse for slaughter on a scale not seen since the Nazis' industrialized murder of European Jews. In January 1979, the Khmer Rouge regime was in turn toppled by a Vietnamese invasion.

ABOVE

Cambodian soldiers escort a blindfolded Khmer Rouge prisoner across a river. The Cambodian army was no more effective than its South Vietnamese counterpart, and the Lon Nol regime might have come to an abrupt end in 1973 had it not been for the support of American B-52 strategic bombers flying "Arclight" missions.

ABOVE
A stack of skulls represents some of the victims of the Khmer Rouge regime whom they murdered following their coming to power in April 1975. The Khmer Rouge rounded up officials of the old regime, and anyone who had contact with the capitalist West. They also herded vast numbers of people from urban areas to forced labour camps in the countryside, without the resources to feed them. Executions amounted to only a small number of the overall death toll, which Amnesty International has estimated at 1.4 million, most due to starvation.

RIGHT
Cambodian troops fire their weapons from behind a rise in the ground. The Cambodian army was equipped with AK-47 automatic rifles supplied from China, the same weapon the Viet Cong and the North Vietnamese Army had as their standard infantry rifle. Ironically, once the United States lent its support to Lon Nol's regime, American arsenals began manufacturing bullets for the AK-47. Quite a few American soldiers wondered whether these bullets might find their way into the chambers of Viet Cong rifles.

THE FALL OF SAIGON

With the end of the American intervention in the Vietnam War in 1973, a brief pause ensued in the fighting in South Vietnam. The Hanoi government intended to prepare for a final offensive that would topple the Saigon regime once and for all and needed to construct roads and stockpile armaments throughout 1973 and 1974. The South Vietnamese knew what was coming, and took advantage of the heavy losses that the North Vietnamese and Viet Cong had suffered in 1972 to launch a series of small-scale offensives during 1973 aimed at recovering lost ground. An uneasy stalemate prevailed in 1974, but in December 1974, however, the North Vietnamese began operations against the town of Phuoc Binh and captured it on 6 January 1975. Rather like a burglar finding an open door, the Hanoi government decided to push in to see what would happen. The result was a stunning collapse of the South Vietnamese regime in just over a hundred days. On 30 April 1975, North Vietnamese tanks drove into Saigon and a war that had lasted 20 years came to an end.

LEFT

Victorious North Vietnamese soldiers sternly ride atop their tank through the streets of Saigon on 30 April 1975. The North Vietnamese and Viet Cong soldiers had endured extremely heavy losses during the war, as the North Vietnamese commander, General Vo Nguyen Giap, made a point of demonstrating the Hanoi government's will to win through his willingness to send hundreds of thousands of his people to death on the battlefield.

ABOVE
An American helicopter loads embassy officials and selected Vietnamese prior to leaving the US embassy in Saigon on 29 April 1975. The Vietnam War has left a huge psychological wound on the American army, whose leaders subsequently pledged themselves to allow "no more Vietnams". To the American armed forces, Vietnam was a war lost by the politicians. For many years after 1975, American military force would only be deployed if the commanding officers were given a large voice in selecting the targets and objectives of the war.

THE MIDDLE EAST

1948–2004

The earliest pictorial representations of warfare are from the Middle East and date to the 3rd millennium BC. As the world entered its sixth millennium of recorded history, the Middle East was still providing visual media with ample scenes of warfare.

In 1918, the Middle East was divided up between Britain and France with little regard for the aspirations of an Arab nationalism that had contributed to the victory over Turkey. Instead of an Arab state with its capital in Damascus replacing the old provinces of the Ottoman empire, Britain and France divided the Middle East between them under the legal jurisdiction of the League of Nations. To complicate matters, the British and French had made commitments to the Zionist political movement. This resulted in a Jewish national home, Israel, being formally established in Palestine by the League's successor, the United Nations, in the aftermath of the Second World War. The existence of Israel and the flight or expulsion of hundreds of thousands of Palestinians became the key issue underlying instability in the Middle East for 40 years after the end of British rule.

Further complications came from the world economy's heavy dependence on oil, a resource in ample supply in the Middle East. Control of oil gave considerable political leverage to many Arab countries, but also made ownership of this scarce commodity a political issue, and eventually into a contributing factor to wars involving Iran, Iraq and Kuwait. This, combined with the challenge of radical Islam to the continuing interventions by non-Islamic states in Middle Eastern affairs, suggests that peace in the Middle East may be a long way off.

LEFT
American troops warily patrol the streets of Baghdad, Iraq, in 2003.

THE 1948–1949 ARAB-ISRAELI WAR

On 15 May 1948, Israel officially became a state under the auspices of the United Nations. The small Jewish population of Palestine during the late nineteenth century had been swollen by a trickle of Jewish immigrants during the first two decades of the twentieth century that broadened into a steady stream during the 1930s. By 1947, some 600,000 Jews lived in Palestine and a small minority of them engaged in active resistance against the British, who administered the region. Neither Jews nor Arabs welcomed the decision by the United Nations to partition Palestine into separate states and, when the day came, war immediately broke out between Israel and its Arab neighbours. The Arabs underestimated the Israeli armed forces, which had experience of war against the British and against Arab guerrillas who had been attacking Jewish settlements. The Arab superiority in weapons was gradually overcome as arms shipments from France and Czechoslovakia arrived. By April 1949, separate armistices with the Arab countries had left Israel in being.

ABOVE
Israeli soldiers, armed with an antiquated Lewis light machine gun, guard a border post during the 1948 war. The Israelis were initially very poorly equipped compared with the Arab armies, and bought weapons from wherever they could find them.

LEFT
Israeli soldiers occupy a captured trench during fighting against the Egyptians near Huleiquat in October 1948. Operation Yoav established the basic outline of the Israeli border with Egypt, which included the existence of the Gaza Strip where Egyptian resistance was strong enough to keep the Israelis out.

LEFT
Israeli soldiers patrol the northern front. The Israeli Defence Force was built from four elements. The Haganah ("defence") was a workers' militia. The Palmach ("shock companies") were permanently mobilized units of the Haganah. Finally, there were some militia groups not associated with the Haganah, such as the Irgun Zevai Leumi (National Military Organization) and the MAHAL foreign volunteers. Women, who were conscripted as well as accepted as volunteers, had combat roles in the initial weeks of fighting, but were eventually withdrawn to support roles.

THE 1956 SUEZ WAR

In July 1956, the Egyptian government seized the Suez Canal. This act brought Egypt into confrontation with the canal's principal shareholders, Britain and France. Relations with France were already strained by Egyptian support for the Algerian nationalists. France was also, at this time, perhaps Israel's closest ally among the world's major powers. Throughout the late summer of 1956, France, Britain and Israel prepared for an attack on Egypt. Israel struck first, on 22 October, with support from the French navy. Nine days later, Anglo-French air strikes were launched against Egypt, and landings to seize the canal were carried out in early November. The Egyptians were in desperate trouble when both the United States and the Soviet Union exerted great diplomatic pressure on all three attacking states to agree to a cease-fire. The Soviets even threatened armed intervention. The peace agreement that was imposed left the canal in Egyptian hands, but made some concessions to increase the security of Israel.

ABOVE
Israeli troops in training in 1956, advancing under the cover of smoke. The Israelis were adept at using manoeuvre both strategically and tactically in their wars with Arab states, in order to minimize the risk of casualties, a high priority with Israel's limited population.

ABOVE
British troops celebrate a successful landing at Port Said, during the 1956 Suez War. The landings were an extremely efficient combined-arms operation, but the Egyptians were unable to put up much of a fight, with much of their army having been engaged and destroyed by the Israeli operations in the Sinai.

THE SIX-DAY WAR OF 1967

During 1965–1967, Israel experienced a growing number of guerrilla raids by Palestinian Arab exiles based in neighbouring Arab states. Rhetoric in those countries increasingly threatened the state of Israel with eradication by military action. In this climate, Israel prepared to attack its neighbours and eliminate the danger. The Israeli onslaught came on 5 June 1967. An initial air strike was highly successful, and command of the air passed to the Israelis within a few hours. The main Israeli blow fell against the Egyptians in the Sinai, and it took three days of fighting to cross the peninsula and reach the Suez Canal. Jerusalem was secured for Israel on 7 June, as well as a border along the River Jordan. Both Syria and Israel initially maintained a defensive posture along the Golan, but Israeli troops struck hard on 9 June, and in a little more than a day secured the heights. Israel had won a remarkable victory in a short space of time.

ABOVE
Israeli paratroops celebrate their victory in Jerusalem in front of the Dome of the Rock in 1967. Fighting in the Old City was intense and difficult, because of a fear of causing damage to the historic centre through artillery bombardment or air strikes.

BELOW
A wrecked Egyptian MiG fighter lies on the ground at El Arish airport. The initial air strike at the outset of the war was vital to their success.

THE OCTOBER WAR OF 1973

The Six-Day War had humiliated the Arab states. They re-equipped their forces with considerable assistance from the Soviet Union, and prepared for another round in the war with Israel. On 6 October 1973, Syria and Egypt, with large-scale support from other Arab countries, launched attacks into the Sinai and the Golan Heights. On both fronts, the Israelis were forced to give ground, and the situation in the Golan became very desperate. The Syrians threatened a major breakthrough, and it required substantial reinforcements and heavy Israeli air strikes to blunt their thrusts. Israel then went on the offensive in the north. The Israelis appeared to be threatening the Syrian capital, Damascus, when they halted their offensive on 13 October. The Israelis now shifted their attacks to the Sinai, where the Egyptians tried to spoil them by launching an assault of their own on 14 October. The largest tank battle since Kursk in 1943 now took place, and the Egyptians were beaten. The Israelis then pushed across the Suez Canal, and superpower intervention forced all sides to accept a cease-fire.

LEFT

Israeli Centurions and a Sherman tank manoeuvre during the 1973 war. The armour battles in the Sinai and along the Golan Heights were the largest since the Second World War.

ABOVE

Egyptian troops hold aloft a portrait of President Anwar el-Sadat, as they celebrate their successful crossing of the Suez Canal. The use of high-pressure water hoses proved an ingenious engineering solution to breaching the sand wall built by the Israelis along their side of the canal bank. The actions here restored some prestige to Egyptian forces, who had been humiliated by the easy Israeli victory in the Six-Day War.

ABOVE

A teenage Iranian soldier shows the strain of combat. The Iranian army had been badly affected by the revolution, and employed clumsy tactics during their offensives. In many respects, the tactics of the Iran-Iraq War were a throwback to the First World War.

THE IRAN-IRAQ WAR

The Iranian Revolution of 1979 established a Shi'ite Islamic fundamentalist regime in one of the major regional powers in the Middle East. Concerns about Iranian influence on Shi'ite Iraqis and urging from Western regimes fearful of the influence of Islamic fundamentalism on the Middle East led to Iraq's invasion of Iran on 22 September 1980. The attack was a failure, as it became bogged down in fighting over the cities of Abadan and Khorramshahr. In 1982, an Iranian offensive recovered most of the territory lost in 1980–1981, and the war became a stalemate of long-range artillery duels and small-scale tactical offensives. The Iranian offensives were marked by costly "human wave" attacks, while the Iraqis used chemical weapons to counter the numerical advantage of the Iranians. In 1988, the Iraqis began bombing Iranian cities and launched a major offensive that achieved some success. The Iranians offered peace talks, Iraq agreed and the war ended with little to show in profit for either side.

ABOVE
Iraqi soldiers in combat during the 1984 offensives. The absence of any natural cover meant that engineering took on great significance in the conflict: bulldozers were used to create artificial obstacles to defend key positions.

THE LEBANON 1975–2000

In 1970, thousands of Palestinian refugees were expelled from Jordan and found refuge in the Lebanon, a state with a delicate balance between its Christian and Muslim Arab population. The Christians were in the minority, although they controlled much of the political establishment. A combustible mixture of angry Palestinians, resentful Muslim Lebanese and fearful Christians exploded in an ugly civil war in1975. Syrian troops occupied parts of the country in 1976, while Israel briefly invaded in 1978. In 1981, the Palestinians began attacking Israel from bases in the Lebanon, and a full-scale invasion by Israel in 1982 brought the eviction of the Palestinian leadership, a short war with Syria and massacres of Palestinian refugees by Christian militia. That year, a multinational force drawn from France, Italy, Britain and the United States attempted to establish peace, but fighting repeatedly broke out between the Lebanese, and against foreign forces. The multinational force was withdrawn in 1984. A negotiated settlement brought the civil war to an end in 1991, but attacks on Israeli forces continued until Israel withdrew in 2000.

LEFT

Israeli armoured vehicles line a Beirut street during the evacuation of the Palestine Liberation Organization in August 1982. Operation "Peace for Galilee" and the subsequent Israeli occupation of part of the Lebanon seriously harmed Israel's international reputation.

LEFT
US Marines dig casualties out of the barracks wrecked by a suicide bomber in October 1983. A similar attack was conducted against French barracks nearby. The multinational force was supposed to keep the peace during an attempt to get Syrian and Israeli forces to withdraw from the Lebanon, but Syria's refusal to accept the terms of this agreement condemned it to failure, while the presence of Western troops – apparently in place of Israeli troops – only encouraged attacks by Islamic radicals that were opposed to such Western intervention.

ABOVE
Shi'ite Amal militiamen fire an RPG-7 at the Palestinian refugee camp of Sabra in 1986. Conflicts such as the Lebanese Civil War and the attacks on Israeli forces in the southern security zone are dominated by part-time soldiers, many of whom probably lack any formal military training, but are shown how to use a weapon, and then sent off to take a few pot shots at the enemy.

THE SOVIET OCCUPATION OF AFGHANISTAN, 1979–1989

In April 1978, a troubled dictatorship in Afghanistan was toppled by a communist-organized coup. The new regime immediately turned to the Soviet Union for help, but Afghan communists were sharply divided between two factions, and the Soviets initially preferred not to be too closely involved. The Iranian Revolution in 1979 changed this stance, as Islam became the main uniting force among those opposed to the communist regime. As civil war threatened, the Soviets invaded in late 1979. In fact, their invasion removed a hard-line government, in the hope that a less ideological regime might reduce support for fundamentalist Islam. However, these fine distinctions were lost on the wider world, and the United States instead lent support to the Islamic fundamentalist guerrillas, the mujahadeen. The Soviet Union became trapped in its own version of Vietnam, an unpopular guerrilla war that seemed unwinnable. The Red Army withdrew in 1989, and the Afghan regime collapsed after a further three years of civil war. The fundamentalists had won.

ABOVE

An elderly mujahadeen fighter trains with a Stinger guided anti-aircraft missile launcher, supplied by the United States. These weapons shifted the balance of power in the conflict back towards the Afghan resistance, who previously had no real answer to the Soviet helicopter gunships.

RIGHT
A Soviet soldier sits atop his armoured personnel carrier while a Mi-24 Hind attack helicopter flies past. The Red Army had emphasized mechanized warfare through most of its history, but massed tank formations were of little use in the mountainous terrain of Afghanistan. Instead, the helicopter gunship came to the rescue of Soviet armoured units, offering a mobile fire platform from which to engage mobile mujahadeen occupying ambush positions in the rugged terrain.

THE FIRST GULF WAR (DESERT STORM)

In August 1990, Iraq invaded and occupied Kuwait, a consequence of a complicated border dispute that stretched back to the defeat of the Ottoman Empire in 1918, but more immediately of the massive foreign debt accumulated by Iraq during the war with Iran, a part of which Iraq demanded that Kuwait should pay. The invasion was condemned by international institutions, and a coalition of 34 countries, headed by the United States, assembled a substantial military and naval presence in Saudi Arabia and the Persian Gulf. In January 1991, the coalition launched a month-long campaign of air bombardment that targeted Iraqi air defences, its ability to support an army in Kuwait and its economy. In response, the Iraqis fired rockets at Israel, a country that had remained scrupulously neutral. On 24 February, the coalition launched its land offensive, and in three days had swept the Iraqis out of Kuwait. Uprisings against Saddam Hussein followed in Iraq, but these were not sufficiently supported by the coalition, and were brutally suppressed by the Iraqi regime.

ABOVE
A US Navy E-2C AWACS aircraft prepares to take off from the USS *Theodore Roosevelt*. AWACS aircraft play a key role in modern air warfare by bringing airborne command-and-control facilities along with a mission.

LEFT
A Royal Air Force Tornado, armed with Air-Launched Anti-Radar Missiles, flies into a combat zone during the First Gulf War. The initial stage of a modern air campaign involves attacking enemy air defences with such missiles. Without effective air defence to threaten them, attacking aircraft can fly at medium altitude, the most suitable height for deploying precision bombing using guided munitions.

LEFT
The pinpoint accuracy of modern guided weapons is shown by the damage to these Iraqi installations, destroyed during the 1991 air campaign. Baghdad and other Iraqi cities were relatively untouched structurally by the bombing. But its effectiveness was far superior to the mass area bombing used during the Second World War, as Baghdad lost electrical and sanitation equipment vital to modern urban life, while the Iraqi high command were deprived of the ability to communicate with their forces through damage to telephone networks and radio broadcasts.

ABOVE
Two US helicopter gunships fly across the desert during Operation Desert Storm. The coalition forces' helicopters were able to fly freely and attack Iraqi troop and vehicle concentrations wherever they could be found, thanks to their command of the air won in the initial stages of the air campaign.

43C

LEFT
A British Army Sultan command vehicle advances with the 7th Armoured Division. Iraqi resistance to the coalition forces was largely limited to attempting to cover their lines of retreat from Kuwait back into Iraq. The major battles of the war occurred at 73 Easting and Medina Ridge, both decisive coalition victories.

THE 2003 INVASION OF IRAQ (SECOND GULF WAR)

The sole support the coalition gave to the Iraqi uprisings after the First Gulf War took the form of enforcing no-fly zones, and carrying out periodic bombings. Economic sanctions were imposed, and a system of weapons inspections was established to search for Iraq's alleged chemical and biological warfare apparatus. After the al-Qaeda terrorist attacks on the United States in September 2001, the American government claimed that Saddam Hussein was amassing chemical and biological weapons and that he was in league with Islamic terrorists. In order to remove this threat, the United States and Britain invaded Iraq on 20 March 2003. Amphibious landings were made in the south of the country, while mechanized units advanced steadily northward from Kuwait on Baghdad. Some Iraqi units fought fiercely, but the country's army was effectively overrun by 15 April 2003. A lengthy occupation has subsequently seen US forces capture Saddam Hussein, but they have suffered heavier casualties than were experienced during the war itself. No chemical or biological weapons have ever been found, nor any clear links with al-Qaeda.

ABOVE
The charred remains of Iraqi soldiers killed during bombing attacks on retreating Iraqi forces along the road from Kuwait to Iraq lie amid the wreckage of their weapons. The route was turned into a free-fire zone for coalition aircraft.

ABOVE
Lightning strikes in the desert near US M1A1 Abrams tanks in the desert. The advance into Iraq was conducted at high speed, without the normal US regard for secure supply lines, and was delayed only by a sandstorm on 24 March.

OVERLEAF
Clouds of smoke billow over Baghdad during one of the coalition strikes at the outset of the 2003 invasion of Iraq. As in the First Gulf War, precision attacks were used to isolate Iraqi military and political command centres from their troops in the field. On this occasion, an intense effort was made to determine the whereabouts of the Iraqi president, Saddam Hussein, and kill him by means of a well-placed air or missile strike.

ABOVE
An Iraqi soldier celebrates the destruction of a US army tank during the fighting in Baghdad in April 2003. The Iraqi forces were unable to mount a co-ordinated defence of their country, in part owing to the success of the air campaign, and in part because of the pace of operations conducted by the Americans in their advance on the capital.

ABOVE
US troops take cover behind a Hummer vehicle as a patrol comes under sniper fire. The American army suffered more casualties in the two years following the occupation of Iraq than during the actual campaign. However, in the absence of a network of bases required to sustain a successful guerrilla campaign, it seems unlikely that the Americans will be evicted from Iraq through military action against its forces there.

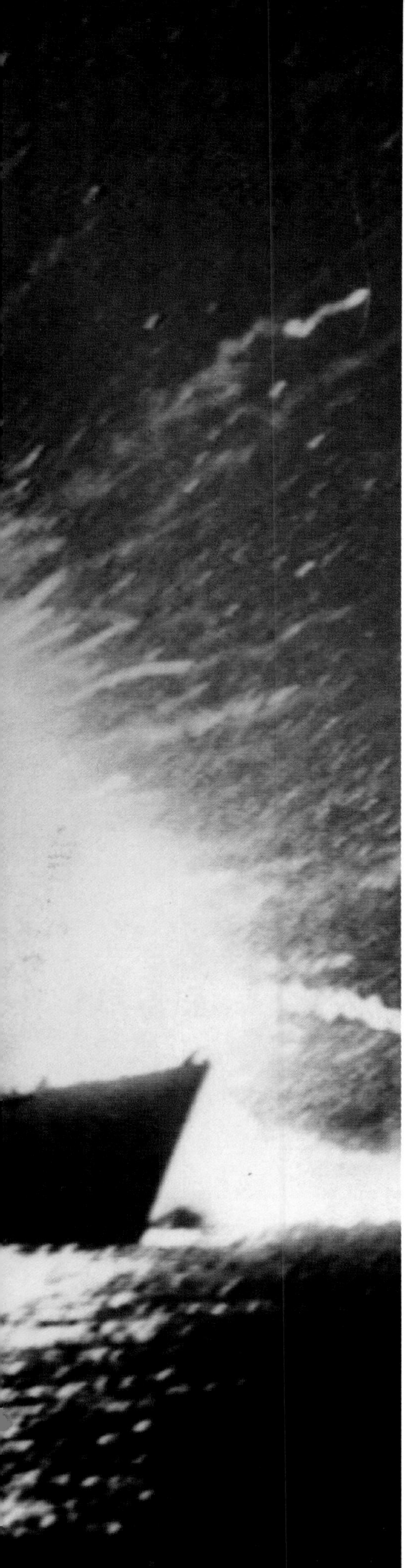

A WORLD AT WAR

1965–2004

Little more than a hundred years after the end of the Crimean War, the world had changed dramatically. The great European empires were almost entirely gone, and a host of new countries sought to live within borders that had been drawn up by outsiders. The great European wars of the twentieth century had produced two major winners. One, the United States, had not been numbered among the Great Powers in 1854; the other, the Soviet Union, had inherited much of the Tsarist Russian empire's strategic policy. The changes served as a stimulus to new patterns of conflict. The small wars that erupted utilized any weapons that could be bought or stolen by the combatants, and made little technological contribution to the art of warfare.

The most significant conflicts have arisen in three regions. In Africa and the Balkans, ethnic rivalries have been the main stimulus for conflict. In both places, borders were not necessarily drawn logically. Especially in the Balkans, the intermingling of peoples of different faiths or languages – and sometimes both – created a degree of instability that, in the absence of the rule of law, could only be resolved through tremendous suffering.

The third region of conflict, Latin America, spawned a different sort of war to those arising in Africa. Civil wars have always been endemic in many of the Central and South American countries. Castro's victory in Cuba created a new front in the Cold War, one vigorously exploited by the élites of these countries who now found an ideological ally in the United States that would support their reluctance to make much-needed social reforms.

LEFT
A weapons magazine explodes aboard HMS *Antelope*, destroying the Royal Navy frigate, on 23 May 1982, during the Falklands War between Britain and Argentina. One member of a two-man bomb disposal team died attempting to defuse the bomb that started the chain of explosions during which this photograph was taken.

AFRICA

Warfare has been a nearly constant feature of Sub-Saharan African history since European countries began the process of decolonization. Some conflicts have their origins in the borders drawn by European rulers, who often had little regard to the region's traditional political organizations. Others have resulted from conflicts over natural resources. But the greatest number have been civil wars. The most savage of all these wars was the ethnic genocide in Rwanda in 1994, a war that later spilled over into the Democratic Republic of Congo. Seven nations have been involved in fighting there since 1998. One of the longest-running conflicts has been in the Sudan, between the Arab-influenced north and the south. This first broke out in 1955, and an agreement ending it was made in1972. The war flared up again in 1983, and a new peace treaty was signed only in January 2005. The dictatorship of Idi Amin in Uganda was overthrown by an invasion from Tanzania in 1979. These conflicts have done little to advance the technology of war, as for the most part they are fought by regimes that lack the scientific and industrial infrastructure, and the financial resources, needed to research and fund such developments. Unfortunately, this limitation does nothing to reduce the horror and misery suffered by the victims of these conflicts.

FAR LEFT
A Nigerian soldier, grenade dangling dangerously by its pin from his hand, guards women and children prisoners from the Ibo tribe during the Biafran War (1967–1970). The war was fought over an attempt by the Ibo to secede from Nigeria, with Biafra having control of Nigeria's considerable oil resources. Some African countries recognized Biafran independence, but most sided with Britain and the Soviet Union in supporting the Nigerian federal government.

LEFT
A child soldier stares sternly at the camera. A civil war broke out in Sierra Leone in 1991. In spite of a UN-sponsored peace agreement, and the presence of 17,000 UN peace-keepers, the violence continues, with widespread use of child soldiers. Children are popular recruits to armies in many African conflicts, because of their willingness to take excessive risks.

LEFT
British marines march (they called it "yomping") on Port Stanley. British forces landed in San Carlos Water, some distance from the Falklands' capital, where there was a suitable anchorage for large numbers of ships. They then marched across East Falkland to defeat the largely conscript Argentine garrison in a series of night actions. It was a demonstration of the superiority of professional soldiers against short-term conscripts.

RIGHT
Salvadoran soldiers patrol through a village. The war in El Salvador had its origins in issues of land and wealth distribution. Marxist-inspired guerrillas fought a conflict that lasted 12 years, from 1979 to 1992. The war was marked by massacres of peasants, and by death squads that assassinated even the country's Catholic primate, Archbishop Oscar Romero. In spite of these human rights violations, the Reagan administration in the United States provided substantial support to the Salvadoran government.

THE FALKLANDS/MALVINAS WAR

On 2 April 1982, Argentine commandos landed near Port Stanley, the town that served as the administrative centre for the Falkland Islands (known as the Malvinas to Spanish speakers). For over a century, the control of the islands had been a matter of dispute between Argentine and British governments. The Argentine military regime believed that a military invasion of the islands would be accepted by the world as a fait accompli, and that the islands would become Argentine through subsequent negotiations. The British government, however, under Prime Minister Margaret Thatcher, chose instead to fight. The resulting war featured a major amphibious operation as the British shipped a small army half-way across the world, the biggest aerial attack on warships since the Second World War and a dramatic cross-country march by British soldiers which ended with the defeat of Argentine forces. Some interesting technical developments took place during the war, including the first sinking of a warship by a submarine propelled by a nuclear reactor, and a demonstration that air-to-surface missiles could be extremely effective against warships. However, in many respects it was a very old-fashioned campaign, effectively a Second-World-War-era operation with updated weaponry.

LATIN AMERICA

After the Cuban Revolution, the states of Latin America became a front-line of the Cold War. Che Guevara attempted to launch a guerrilla movement in Bolivia in the late 1960s. Military coups occurred in Peru, Chile and Argentina. A war between leftists and the government in Colombia broke out. A Maoist-inspired guerrilla movement arose in Peru. In the late 1970s, Central American countries such as Guatemala, El Salvador and Nicaragua became the cockpit of the struggle between leftist guerrillas and US-supported governments. Only in Nicaragua did a guerrilla movement actually secure a victory, but the new government itself became the target of US-supported guerrillas operating from bases in neighbouring countries. The huge revenues from illegal drug smuggling, especially into the United States and Europe, added a new twist to the Cold War, especially in Colombia, where drug money funded both guerrillas and paramilitary militias that fought against them. Fortunately, fighting between states has been limited to one Latin American conflict, the Football War in 1969 between El Salvador and Honduras. Tensions between Chile and Argentina, Colombia and Venezuela, and Colombia and Ecuador never escalated into outright war.

ABOVE
Professor Abimael Guzman, the founder of the Peruvian Shining Path guerrilla movement, behind bars. Guzman was a philosophy professor-turned revolutionary who married Maoist political dogma to traditional indigenous native opposition to the creole ruling class of Peru. Shining Path launched a guerrilla campaign in 1980 to overthrow the government. The movement was crippled, however, in September 1992 when Guzman, and more usefully his computer, were captured by Peruvian anti-terrorist police. The data on the computer enabled the Peruvian government to damage Shining Path almost fatally, although the movement still exists.

BELOW
Guerrillas opposed to Nicaragua's leftist Sandinista government sail down the San Juan River separating Costa Rica and Nicaragua in 1983. The Reagan administration in the US gave strong support to these forces, believing the Sandinistas were sponsoring the leftist guerrillas in El Salvador and that they were intent on forming an alliance with Cuba. The war ended with an agreement in 1988 and elections in 1990, in which the Sandinistas were defeated. The war was most notable for Nicaragua's securing of a World Court judgment law in 1986 declaring the United States in violation of international law. By this time, the Contras were being funded illegally by members of the Reagan administration who, it is assumed, acted without the president's knowledge.

ABOVE
Colombian police examine the scene of a fatal bombing of a police car by leftist rebels in 2004. The war in Colombia began with the insurgency of the Revolutionary Armed Forces of Colombia (FARC) in 1964, who were joined by the National Liberation Army (ELN) in 1966. The causes of the war are fundamentally social inequality and political corruption, but the growth of the Colombian cocaine and other illegal drugs industries has led to a confused situation. In many ways the conflict could now be characterized as a continuation of a civil war between political factions that has plagued the country periodically since 1899. The Colombian guerrillas have, unlike most Latin American insurgents, gained control of significant areas. However, the underdeveloped nature of these areas allows the national economy to function without them.

SOMALIA

The overthrow of the Siad Barre regime in Somalia in 1991 resulted in a total collapse of all central authority in the country. People starved, violence became endemic and in 1992 the United Nations intervened militarily, mainly to ensure the safe delivery of food aid. The force was a multinational one, but its most important element was from the United States. The intervention was not entirely welcome by the Somali factions, and the United Nations attempted to keep some kind of order using military force, which resulted in October 1993 in several military actions, including the engagement between US forces and Somalis in Mogadishu that was recounted in the book and film *Black Hawk Down*. The UN force was withdrawn in 1995, and the country remains divided, with several secessionist states having emerged. The war led to considerable disillusionment in the United States about the effectiveness of United Nations' intervention, and contributed to a reluctance by the US armed forces to commit to subsequent UN operations.

BELOW
US Marines on patrol shortly after the beginning of Operation *Restore Hope* in December 1992. The US armed forces performed well in the operation, although at the time the Battle of Mogadishu was treated in the media as a defeat.

ABOVE
Chechen fighters scamper from cover across a street in Grozny in January 1995. The Russians launched the First Chechen War in late 1994, hoping by swift action to put an end to Chechnya's independence. However, the poor quality of Russian troops, many of whom were conscripts who had gone unpaid for some time, together with the determination of the Chechens, turned the conflict into a quagmire.

CHECHNYA

After the collapse of the Soviet Union at the end of the 1991, its successor, the Russian Federation, faced demands for negotiations on autonomy from several of its constituent states. Most were agreed peaceably, but in Chechnya, near the Caucasus Mountains, a war broke out. The Russian government at first attempted to topple the Chechens' elected regime by supporting an armed uprising by its opponents. When this failed, the Russians attempted a sudden air assault, followed by a rapid advance by its army, the traditional manner of attack by its Soviet predecessor. The Chechen capital Grozny was reduced to rubble, and the Russian army became bogged down in street fighting reminiscent of Stalingrad. The fighting in cities and in the mountainous areas of the country continued for almost two years, until a peace treaty was signed in 1997, which granted continued independence to Chechnya. However, in September 1999, the Russians launched a second, more carefully planned assault, that eventually established Russian military rule over the region. The conflict became one of guerrilla warfare and resulted in terrorist operations such as the Moscow theatre siege of October 2002, and the Beslan school siege in September 2004.

ABOVE
Russian conscripts, such as this young man, bore the brunt of the fighting during both Chechen wars. The soldiers were better prepared and motivated for the second war, which was characterized as an "anti-terrorist" intervention. The fighting continues in the mountains in the south of Grozny, and the Russians have tried very hard to get the fighting in Chechnya regarded in the same light as the US interventions in Afghanistan and Iraq – as part of an international war on Islamic fundamentalist terrorism.

FORMER YUGOSLAVIA

Croatia and Slovenia, former constituent republics of Yugoslavia, seceded from the federation in 1991. In both cases, the Yugoslav army attempted to compel them back into the federation. In both cases the use of military force failed, although the war with Croatia continued intermittently until 1995. In 1992, however, Bosnia voted for independence. Unlike Croatia and Slovenia, no single ethnic group dominated Bosnia, and the war there, which received extensive media coverage, involved mass killings and refugees on a scale not seen in Europe since the Second World War. The Bosnian conflict fed into a fourth war, over the status of Kosovo, a region predominantly Albanian in population. In 1999, an attempt to impose a solution on Yugoslavia led to one of the most remarkable wars in history. The Kosovo War (also known as the Yugoslav War) was conducted by NATO entirely using aircraft. While the Yugoslavs suffered substantial losses in both human and economic terms, not a single NATO serviceman was killed as a result of enemy action. A bombing campaign that lasted three months, and which involved 1,000 aircraft, eventually compelled the Yugoslav government to admit peace-keepers to protect the Albanian Kosovars. However, the war did not have the support of the United Nations, and was unusual for being criticized as much by normally supportive conservative political politicians, as by radicals.

LEFT
Bodies of those killed during the shelling of the Sarajevo marketplace in February 1994 are removed by survivors. The conflict in Bosnia represented a failure of European diplomacy, as European governments declined to intervene to prevent a war that could easily have been avoided by more immediate action.

ABOVE
Craters around the ruins of a Kosovo village mark the intensity of the fire-power unleashed on the largely rural region. The Yugoslav government attempted to drive the Albanian population of the region off the land, and created a huge refugee crisis in neighbouring Bosnia, Albania and Macedonia. The whole sequence of wars over former Yugoslavia displaced tens of thousands of people, as ethnic groups who had previously lived together rediscovered old rivalries dating back centuries.

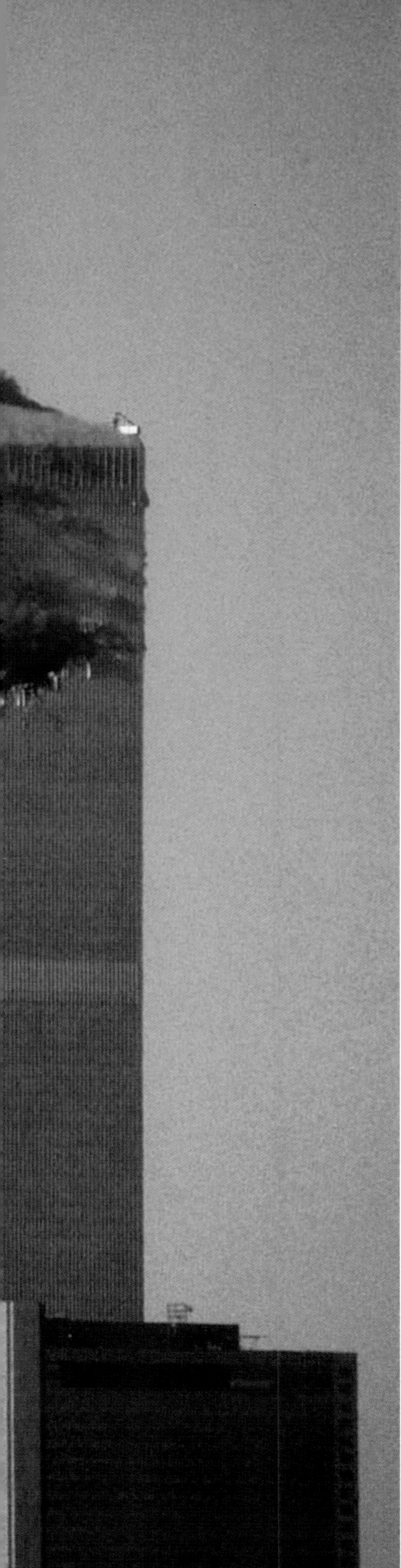

TERRORISM

1971–2004

Terrorism, in this book, is used to mean conflicts in which one side is wholly composed of irregular forces of volunteers fighting against the military or civil institutions of a country they perceive as the enemy. Terrorism has become one of the most visible forms of armed struggle in contemporary media. Indeed, there are some acts of terrorism specifically intended to have a decisive impact on the world's media. The al-Qaeda attacks on the World Trade Center in New York City and the Pentagon in Washington, D.C., are probably the best-known recent examples. They have produced instantly recognizable images which serve as inspiration both to those fighting the terrorists and to the terrorists themselves.

Terrorist warfare is asymmetric. The terrorists may have regular access to small arms and explosives, but not to armour, warships, military aircraft, or heavy artillery. The terrorist arsenal includes improvised weapons such as car bombs, civil aircraft converted into flying bombs, one-shot home-made mortar tubes and sometimes even home-made hand-guns. They do not raise their financial support through taxation, but more normally via donations or robberies. They do not often wear uniforms, and are likely to operate clandestinely.

Fighting terrorism is an awkward problem for military forces. Like guerrillas, terrorists often rely on a sympathetic population to support them in their operations, and distinguishing between a terrorist fighter and a civilian sympathizer is by no means straightforward. Soldiers find themselves turning into policemen with licence to kill, but without necessarily having the training in resorting to violence tempered with a caution that is vital for law enforcement officers.

LEFT
United Air Lines Flight 175 explodes in a fireball as it strikes the South Tower of the World Trade Center, 11 September 2001. The North Tower burns after being struck by American Airlines Flight 11.

NORTHERN IRELAND, 1971–1998

Protestant Northern Ireland, part of the United Kingdom, possessed an avowedly sectarian police force that oppressed the Catholic minority with particular severity in the late 1960s. Unable to control the protest riots, the police required the help of the British army. At the same time, a spilt in the Irish Republican Army produced a Provisional wing, which began to act as a paramilitary defence force for the Catholic community. In February 1971, IRA snipers shot British soldiers for the first time and unleashed a series of snipings, bombings and assassinations.

BELOW

Members of the Provisional IRA parade through the streets. The IRA has a formal military structure, but does not use traditional guerrilla warfare to wage its fight for a united Ireland. The IRA's methods have become the model for terrorist warfare used by irregular forces against a traditional army.

ABOVE

An Israeli sniper takes aim during the Second Intifada, in April 2002. Because of the political consequences of indiscriminate fire against terrorists hiding among civilians, soldiers must take great care in identifying targets before using lethal force.

THE INTIFADAS 1987–2004

The occupation by Israel of the Gaza Strip and the West Bank areas of Palestine since 1967 became the target of a spontaneous uprising of Palestinian Arabs in the last quarter of 1987. It was marked by rioting and acts of civil disobedience that continued at high intensity for four years. However, the Israeli security forces were eventually able to impose some authority on the situation, and violence in the period 1991–93 was at a much lower level. The targets for the riots were Israeli patrols, and the weapons used were rocks, Molotov cocktails, sniper fire and grenades. The Palestinian Liberation Organization, Palestinian Islamic Jihad and Hamas were able to impose a degree of organization on the rioting. The First Intifada was ended by the Oslo Accords of 1993, which provided for the establishment of a Palestinian Authority and a gradual withdrawal of Israeli forces. The accords were not fully implemented, which resulted in a renewed outbreak in September 2000.

ABOVE
A Palestinian fighter launches a rifle grenade in the direction of an Israeli army patrol. Terrorists must rely on concealment and mobility to succeed in their attacks on armed forces, whose firepower tends to be considerably superior.

AL-QAEDA'S WAR ON THE UNITED STATES

Al-Qaeda is a loose confederation of Muslim fundamentalists who aim to liberate the Muslim world from a materialist culture whose focus lies in the West. It grew out of the war against the Soviet Union in Afghanistan, but has shifted the main target of its attacks to the United States. Its leader, Osama bin Laden, a wealthy Saudi Arabian, formally declared war on America in 1998, but had allegedly been involved in terrorist acts committed against United States forces prior to that. In 1996, bin Laden established training bases in Afghanistan, and in 1998 directed attacks on two US embassies in East Africa. The Americans responded with bombing raids against Sudan, where bin Laden had previously been resident, and Afghanistan, and a campaign of surveillance and intelligence gathering aimed at locating and killing him. In the end, al-Qaeda was able to strike first, with its attacks using hijacked airliners in New York City and Washington, D.C., on 11 September 2001.

RIGHT
A casualty is evacuated from the ruins of the US embassy in Kenya in August 1998. Most of the victims of al-Qaeda's bombing were local civilians.

ABOVE
Water flows into the damaged hull of the USS *Cole*, the target of an attack by suicide bombers in the port of Aden in October 2000. Suicide bombing with conventional explosives has yet to prove an effective means of winning a war, since few people have the fanatical determination needed, and the attackers would have to number in the thousands in order to achieve a meaningful victory.

ABOVE
Wreckage litters "Ground Zero" at the World Trade Center in New York in this dramatic photograph by James Nachtwey, after the collapse of the Twin Towers on 11 September 2001. The use of airliners as missiles was an innovative and unexpected move by al Qaeda terrorists; the success of the attack apparently even astounded al Qaeda's leadership.

OPERATION ENDURING FREEDOM, 2001–2004

Following the 11 September 2001 attacks, the United States prepared and carried out an invasion of Afghanistan. Bombing began on 7 October 2001, and the forces of the Northern Alliance, opposed to the ruling Muslim fundamentalist Taliban government in Afghanistan, began receiving military support from America. In November, the capital Kabul fell, and in December the Taliban leader, Mullah Omar, retreated to a mountain hideout. Meanwhile, US ground forces targeted the Tora Bora cave complex in the east of the country, where it was believed al-Qaeda leader Osama bin Laden was hiding. The complex fell in December, but bin Laden apparently escaped, and went into hiding, most probably in either Afghanistan or Pakistan, from where he has continued to send messages to his supporters. Resistance by Taliban forces against the US invasion and the subsequent democratically elected republic continues in Afghanistan, a state that historically has suffered from a lack of a strong central government, with much power devolved to local leaders.

BELOW
US Special Forces soldiers sit in the back of a pick-up truck on the streets of Kandahar in December 2001. The War on Terror will see a larger role for Special Forces than has been traditional in the US military, which historically has been sceptical of the value of such élite units.

ABOVE
Soldiers of the Princess Patricia's Canadian Light Infantry march on patrol in Afghanistan in March 2002. Bahraini, British, Danish, Dutch, French, German, Japanese, Jordanian, New Zealand, Romanian, Russian, Australian, Italian and Norwegian troops have also participated in Afghan operations, illustrating a far greater range of support than the March 2003 invasion of Iraq received.

TERRORISM IN THE TWENTY-FIRST CENTURY

After the 9/11 attacks on the United States, terrorism moved to the centre stage of military conflict. At the forefront of these attacks was Islamic fundamentalist terrorism. The causes of Islamic terrorism are many, but can be summarised as a continued resentment at the Palestinian situation, and the refusal of most Muslim societies to accommodate the social changes created by Western capitalism, especially in the areas of justice and human rights. For the targets of such terrorism, the sheer scale of probable casualties in a terrorist incident has put great emphasis on obtaining prior warning of possible attacks. In military terms, special forces able to intervene with minimum risk to hostages are most prominent.

ABOVE
A scene from a videotape broadcast by a Russian television channel during the seizure of a theatre in Moscow, shows Chechen fighters with explosives strapped to their bodies. On 23 October 2002, a large group of Chechen fighters, officially estimated at 33, took hostage the entire audience attending a play. After three days of negotiations, Russian special forces pumped the theatre full of an aerosol anaesthetic gas and then stormed the building. They shot all the Chechen fighters they could find, while the gas killed over a hundred of the hostages.

ABOVE
US soldiers clear the wreckage of the Canal Hotel in Baghdad in August 2003. The hotel was blown up by a truck bomb which targeted the headquarters of the United Nations in Iraq. The explosion killed the UN Secretary-General's special envoy to Iraq, Sérgio Vieira de Mello, and 21 other people, most of them humanitarian workers. Whether the attack was carried out by Islamic radicals or pro-Saddam Hussein Ba'athists has never been clear.

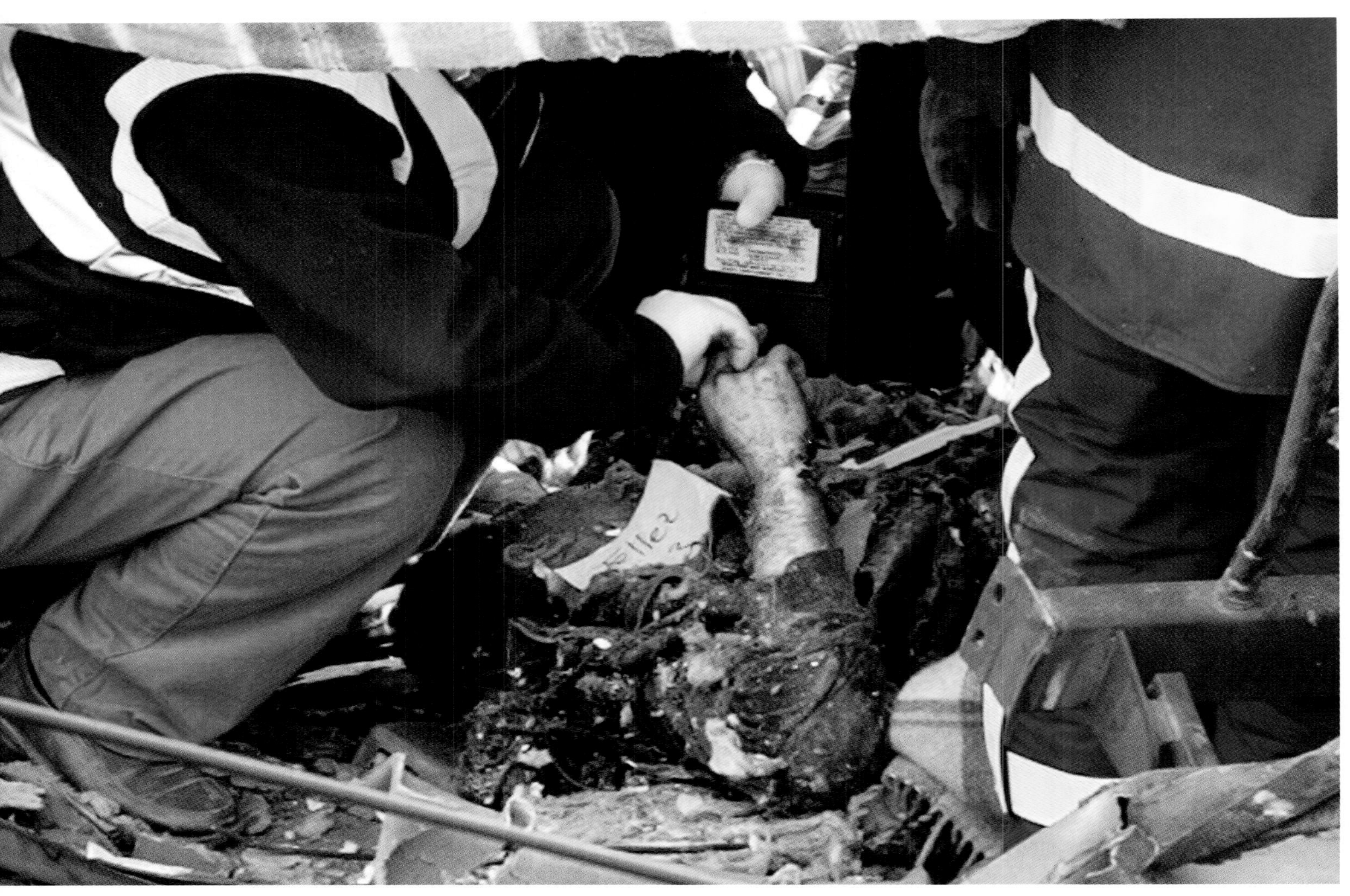

ABOVE

Rescue workers fingerprint a body found in the wreckage of a commuter train in Madrid on 11 March 2004. Ten explosions took place during the morning rush hour, killing nearly 200 people and wounding nearly 2,000. The Spanish government immediately blamed the Basque terrorist movement ETA. However, as police studied the evidence, it soon became clear that ETA was not responsible. Instead, the attacks were the responsibility of a Moroccan-based Islamic fundamentalist group.

ABOVE
A Russian special forces commando carries a released baby away from the Beslan school before the disastrous end to this hostage crisis. A whole school was seized by the Chechens who rigged it with bombs. When one of these was detonated, possibly accidentally, on the third day of the siege, 3 September 2004, the security forces stormed the building and by nightfall had killed or captured all the hostage-takers. Over 300 civilians, many of them children, were killed in the operation.

INDEX

A

Abd-el-Krim 159
Adams, Eddie 318
Afghanistan 355–6, 389, 392, 393
Africa 52–4, 58, 372–3
aircraft 97, 110, 120, 133, 180, 185, 195, 210, 214, 224, 226–7, 240–1, 242, 250, 252, 254–5, 304, 309, 310–11, 321, 345, 356, 357, 358–9, 361
aircraft carriers 144, 209
Albania 87
Alexandria 55
Algeria 280–2
Alost 95
al-Qaeda 364, 389–91
American Civil War 10, 26–49
Anglo-Zulu War 52–4
Antelope, HMS 370–1
anti-aircraft weapons 116–17, 190, 355
Arabi Revolt 55–6
Arab-Israeli War 340–1
Argentina 374, 375
Argus, HMS 144
Arnhem 258
artillery 74–5, 88–9, 100, 108, 115, 122–3, 145, 175, 201, 228, 229, 230, 231, 238, 246–7, 288, 308
Atlantic, Battle of the 194–9
atomic bomb 270
Australian troops 107, 130–1
Austria 72, 104
Austro-Hungary 87, 113
Austro-Prussian War 73

B

Baghdad 338–9, 366–7, 395
Balaclava 21
Balkan Wars 87–9
balloons 44, 65, 78, 184
Bangladesh 286–7
Barbarossa 200–5
Batista, Fulgencio 298
Battle of the Somme, *The* 124
Beato, Felice 13, 23, 24, 25
Beaton, Cecil 11, 13
Belgium 92, 94, 95, 98, 135, 142
Biafran War 372
Big Foot 59
Bismarck, German battleship 196–7
Bismarck, Otto von 75
Boer War 61–5
Bolivia 160–1, 375, 382
Bourrasque, French destroyer 182
Boxer Rebellion 66–9
Brady, Matthew 13, 32
Britain 25, 52, 55, 61–5, 92, 94, 106, 109, 112, 126, 127, 128, 133, 136, 188, 194, 235, 273, 274, 277–9, 374
Britain, Battle of 183–7
British troops 19, 20, 62–3, 90–1, 96, 98, 102–3, 108, 116–17, 118, 119, 122–3, 130–1, 138, 142–3, 146–7, 178, 213, 232, 258, 343, 374
Brockliss, J. Frank 95
Brusilov offensive 113
Bulgaria 87, 88–9
Bulge, Battle of the 258, 259
Burma 206, 208
Burrough, Sir Harold, Rear-Admiral 217

C

Cairo, USS 41
Cambodia 322–5, 332–5
Canadian troops 128, 231, 243, 393
Capa, Robert 6, 13, 15, 162, 243
Castro, Fidel 298, 299
Chaco War 160–1
Chattanooga, Tennessee 35
Chechnya 380–1, 394, 397
child soldiers 349, 373
Chile 300, 301, 375
China 25, 58, 66–9, 82, 168–9, 206, 334
Christmas Truce 1914 98
Churchill, Winston 106
Cold Wars 290–301
Cole, USS 390
Colombia 375, 378
concentration camps 264, 265
Constellation, USS 331
Coral Sea, Battle of 209
Crete 192–3
Crimean War 8, 17, 18–22
Cuba 79, 298–9
Cumberland Landing 34
Cyrenaica 188–9
Czechoslovakia 300, 340

D

de Gaulle, Charles 174, 249, 280
Delhi 24
Denmark 72, 179
Dieppe 216
Dorsetshire, HMS 197
Dunn, John 53

E

Easter Offensive, Vietnam 328–31
Eben Emael 180
Egypt 55–6, 209, 341, 342, 343, 345, 347, 348
executions 66–7, 204

F

Falklands War 371, 374
Fenton, Roger 16, 18
Ferdinand, Franz 92
First World War 13, 91–149
Flanders 99
Flynn, Sean 15
Foch, Marshal 148
France 25, 58, 70–1, 78, 94, 114, 149, 238–49, 249, 273, 280–2, 340, 342
Franco-Prussian War 74–8
Franklin, USS 266
French Foreign Legion 50–1, 58, 275
French Indochina War 274–6
French troops 94, 101, 113, 115, 121, 174, 175, 274, 280–1

G

Gallipoli 106, 107
German troops 98, 99, 113, 140–1, 179, 180, 192–3, 222, 223, 259
Germany 72, 87, 92, 94, 98, 106, 109, 112, 113, 114, 126, 127, 128, 133, 141, 163, 172, 173, 174, 178, 179, 188, 200–5, 220, 224–7, 228, 231, 232, 233, 235, 238, 258–65
Graf Spee, German cruiser 176–7
Grant, Ulysses S., General 36–7
Greece 87, 188, 191, 291
Grozny 380
Guatemala 300, 375
Guernica 165
guerrilla movement 375–8
Guevara, Che 298, 375
Gulf War, First 13, 357–63
Gulf War, Second 364–9
Gurkhas 11
Guzman, Abimael 37

H

Hiroshima 270
Hitler, Adolf 93, 171, 179, 200, 220, 238, 252, 258, 263
Hood, HMS 196
hostages 395, 397
Hussein, Saddam 357, 364, 365

I

Iceland 199
Inchon 293
India 23–4, 253, 273
Indian troops 139, 283
Indochina 58, 274–6
Indo-Pakistani Wars 283–8
Intifadas 387–8
Intrepid, block ship 142
Invincible, HMS 112
Iphigenia, block ship 142
IRA, Provisional 386
Iran 349–50, 355
Iraq 13, 150–1, 338–9, 349–50, 357, 361, 363, 364–9, 395
Ireland 155–8, 386
Israel 340–1, 342, 344, 351, 387
Italy 87, 171, 188, 231–3
Iwo Jima 266, 267, 268–9

J

Japan 82–5, 168–9, 206–8, 209, 210, 253, 255, 256, 257, 266–71
Jellicoe, Sir John 109, 112
Johnson, L. B. 320
Juno beach 243
Jutland 109–12

K

Kandahar 392
Kashmir 283
Kenya 277, 278–9, 389
Khmer Rouge 332, 333
Kirkuk 138
Korea 291, 292–7
Kosovo 382, 383
Kundt, Hans, General 160
Kursk 228–30
Kuwait 357

L

Laden, Osam bin a 389, 392
Ladoga, Lake 221
Lawrence, T. E. 136, 137
leaflet dropping 178
Lebanon 351–4
Leningrad 221
Lexington, USS 209
London 133, 251
Lucknow 23
Lusitania, RMS 105

M

MacArthur, Douglas, General 257, 271
Macedonia 87
Madrid 396
Maginot Line 174
Maine, USS 79
Malaya 206, 207, 277
Marianas 253
Maxim, Sir Hiram 57
Mesopotamia 108, 138, 139
Messines Ridge 130
Mexico 58, 59
Middle East 136–9, 338–69
Midway, Battle of 209, 210
Mogadishu 379
Monitor, USS 40
Montgomery, Bernard, General 209, 258
Morocco 159, 396
mujahadeen 355
Mulberries 238
Munich 93
Musashi, Japanese battleship 256
Muslims 351, 354, 389, 394
Mussolini, Benito 188, 252

N

NATO 382
Nicaragua 375, 377
Nigeria 372
Nixon, Richard 320, 322, 326
Nol, Lon, General 322, 332
Normandy 10–12, 238–49
Northern Ireland 386
Norway 179

O

Omaha beach 243
Operation *"Peace for Galilee"* 351
Operation *Desert Storm* 357–63
Operation *Enduring Freedom* 392–3
Operation *Lam Son* 327
Operation *Restore Hope* 379
Operation *Torch* 217, 218–19
Operation *Yoav* 341
O'Sullivan, Timothy 38–9

P

Pacific War 253–7
Page, Tim 15
Pakistan 283–8
Palermo 171
Palestine 340, 387, 388
Paraguay 160–1
Paris 70–1, 78, 149, 249
Pearl Harbor 206
periscopes 101
Peru 375, 376
Philippines 60, 257
Phoney War 172–8
Phuc, Kim 330
Plains Wars 59
PLUTO 238
Poland 172–8, 233
Port Arthur 82, 84
Port Moresby 209
Port Said 343
Port Stanley 374
prisoners 90–1, 166–7, 188–9, 299
Prussia 72, 73–8

Q

Queen Mary, HMS 111

R

radar 183, 238
Rhodesia 277, 289
Ribbentrop, Joachim von 172
Riff War 159
River Clyde, SS 106
Robertson, James 19, 22
Romania 87
Roosevelt, Theodore 81
Rouen 94
Royal Air Force 224, 358–9
Russia 18, 71, 87, 113, 132, 200
Russian Civil War 152–3
Russian Federation 380–1
Russo-Japanese War 82–5
Rutland, Frederick 110
Rwanda 372

S

el-Sadat, Anwar 348
Saigon 336–7
Saipan 253, 255
El Salvador 375, 377
Sarajevo 382
Schleswig-Holstein War 72
Second Opium War 25
Second World War 10–12, 171–271
Seoul 291, 293
Serbia 87
Sevastapol, siege of 16, 22
Sierra Leone 373
Sino-Japanese War 168–9
Six-Day War 344–5
Solomon Islands 215
Somalia 379
Somme, battle of the 113, 125
Soviet troops 205, 220, 228, 229, 230, 258, 262, 263, 356
Soviet Union 200–5, 220–3, 228–30, 291, 292, 300, 342, 355
Spain 59, 60, 79–81, 159, 396
Spanish Civil War 162–7
Stalin, Joseph 172, 291
Stalingrad 220–3
submarine warfare 105, 126–7, 194, 195, 235–7
Sudan 372
Suez War 342–3
suicide bombers 13, 352–3, 384–5, 390, 391, 394, 395
Sumter, Fort 28
Sweden 179
Syria 347, 351, 353

T

Taliban 392
tanks 125, 161, 163, 191, 200, 201, 212, 216, 228, 292, 346–7, 362–3, 365
Taranto 188
Tarawa 253
telegraph wagons 48–9
terrorism 13, 384–97
Tet Offensive, Vietnam 14, 317–19, 320
Thatcher, Margaret 374
Theodore Roosevelt, USS 357
Thetis, block ship 142
Thomas, Lowell 137
Thruz, Karl-Heinz, Lieutenant 187
Tientsin 69
Tigris river 108
trench warfare 46, 99, 100, 101, 102–3, 104, 113, 115, 119, 142–3, 230
Tsesarevitch, Russian battleship 83
Turkey 87, 106–8, 136

U

Uganda 372
United Nations 379, 395
United States of America 13, 26–49, 59–60, 71, 79–81, 126, 128, 206, 210, 273, 291, 292, 300, 303, 304, 317, 334, 337, 342, 384–5, 389–91, 392, 394/ *see also* American Civil War
US Army Air Force 226–7
US troops 14, 80, 81, 145, 170–1, 198–9, 215, 218–19, 234–5, 244–5, 246–7, 248, 253, 260, 261, 263, 267, 268–9, 293, 294, 295, 296, 307, 312–13, 314, 315, 316, 319, 322, 325, 326, 338–9, 352–3, 379, 392
Ut, Nick 330

V

V beach 106
Verdun 113, 114
Viet Cong 318, 326, 329
Viet Minh 272–3, 274, 276
Vietnam 14, 273, 302–37
Vimy Ridge, battle of 129
Volturno river 232

W

Women's Royal Naval Service 213
World Trade Center 384–5, 391

Y

Yorktown, USS 254–5
Ypres 103, 135
Yugoslavia, Former 382–3

Z

Zeebrugge 142
Zhukov, Georgi, Field Marshal 228
Zimbabwe 289
Zulus 52–3

CREDITS

The publishers would like to thank the following sources for their kind permission to reproduce the pictures in the book.

2–3: Getty Images/Alphonse Liebert; 4: Corbis / Bettmann; 6: © Magnum Photos Ltd./Robert Capa; 11: IWM (IB 283); 14: Corbos/Bettmann; 16: Corbis/Hulton-Deutsch Collection; 18: Getty Images/Hulton Archive; 19: Getty Images/Roger Fenton; 20: Getty Images/Hulton Archive; 21: Getty Images/Roger Fenton; 22: Getty Images/Robertson; 23: Getty Images/Felice Beato; 24: Getty Images/Felice Beato; 25: Getty Images/Felice Beato; 26–27: Tennessee State Library; 28: USAMHI; 29: USAMHI; 30: John Hess; 31: USAMHI; 32: Civil War Times Illustrated/CWTI Collection; 33: USAMHI; 34: Library of Congress; 35: USAMHI; 36–37: U.S. National Archives & Records Administration; 38–39: Library of Congress; 40: Library of Congress; 41: USAMHI; 42–43: U.S. National Archives & Records Administration; 44: Library of Congress; 45: USAMHI; 46: (bottom) Library of Congress; 47: Corbis/Bettmann; 48–49: Corbis/Bettmann; 50–51: Getty Images/Hulton Archive; 52: Topfoto.co.uk; 53: Topfoto.co.uk; 54: Topfoto.co.uk; 55: Getty Images/Hulton Archive; 56: Getty Images/Hulton Archive; 57: Corbis/Bettmann; 58: Getty Images/Hulton Archive; 59: Corbis/Bettmann; 60: Corbis/George C. Dotter; 61: Getty Images/Hulton Archive; 62–63: Getty Images/Reinhold Thiele; 64: Getty Images/Van Hoepen; 65: Getty Images/Hulton Archive; 66–67: Getty Images/Time Life Pictures/Mansell Collection; 68: Getty Images/Hulton Archive; 69: Topfoto.co.uk/Public Record Office/HIP; 70: Corbis/Bettmann; 72: Getty Images/Henry Guttmann; 73: Getty Images/Hulton Archive; 74–75: Getty Images/Alphonse Liebert; 76–77: Getty Images/Henry Guttmann; 78: Corbis/Hulton-Deutsch Collection; 79: Getty Images/Henry Guttmann; 80: Corbis/Bettmann; 81: Corbis/Bettmann; 82: Imperial War Museum (Q 91838); 83: Getty Images/Hulton Archive; 84: Getty Images/Hulton Archive; 85: Corbis/Bettmann; 86–87: Getty Images/Topical Press Agency; 88–89: Getty Images/Topical Press Agency; 90: IWM (Q 4057); 92: IWM (Q 81831); 93: IWM (Q 65860); 94: IWM (HU 71985); 95: IWM (Q 100136); 96: IWM (Q 51506); 97: IWM (HU 67825); 98: IWM (Q 50720); 99: IWM (Q 53538); 100: IWM (Q 78062); 101: Corbis/Hulton-Deutsch Collection; 102: IWM (Q 49750); 104: IWM (HU 68589); 105: IWM (Q 108330); 106: IWM (Q 50473); 107: IWM (Q 13392); 108: (top) IWM (Q 106217); 108: (bottom) IWM (Q 106215); 109: IWM (Q 55499); 110: IWM (Q 82238); 111: IWM (HU 69073); 112: IWM (SP 2468); 113: IWM (Q 23760); 114: IWM (Q 78038); 115: IWM (Q 73413); 116–117: IWM (Q 460); 118: IWM (Q 718); 119: IWM (Q 3990); 120: IWM (Q 106227); 121: IWM (Q 450); 122–123: IWM (Q 5817); 124: IWM (Q 79496); 125: Corbis/Hulton-Deutsch Collection; 126: IWM (Q 20343); 127: IWM (Q 19954); 129: IWM (Q 5095); 130–131: IWM (E AUS 632); 132: IWM (Q 103662); 133: (top) IWM (HU63634); 133: (bottom) IWM (Q 65535); 134: IWM (E AUS 715); 136: IWM (Q 59193); 137: Corbis/Bettmann; 138: IWM (Q 24707); 139: IWM (Q 24707); 140–141: IWM (Q 47997); 142: (bottom left) IWM (Q 49164); 142–143: IWM (Q 72619); 144: Corbis/Hulton-Deutsch Collection; 145: Getty Images/Sgt. J. A. Marshall; 146–147: IWM (Q 95579); 148: IWM (Q 43225); 149: IWM (Q 81860);150–151: Corbis/Bettmann; 152–153: Corbis/Hulton-Deutsch Collection; 154: Corbis; 155: Corbis/Hulton-Deutsch Collection; 156–157: Getty Images/Walshe; 158: Corbis/Hulton-Deutsch Collection; 159: Corbis/Hulton-Deutsch Collection; 160: Corbis/Bettmann; 161: Corbis/Bettmann; 162: © Magnum Photos Ltd./Robert Capa; 163: IWM (HU 34723); 164: Corbis/Hulton-Deutsch Collection; 165: Corbis/Bettmann; 166–167: Corbis/Hulton-Deutsch Collection; 168: IWM (CHN 316); 169: Corbis/Bettmann; 170–171: IWM (GL 885); 172: AKG-Images; 173: IWM (HU 5455); 174: IWM (MH 24390); 175: IWM (HU 86048); 176–177: IWM (A6); 178: IWM (C 826); 179: IWM (NYP 68074); 180–181: IWM (PC 449); 182: IWM (HU 2280); 183: IWM (CH 15173); 184: IWM (CH 1522); 185: IWM (C 5422); 186: IWM (C 189); 187: IWM (HU 23746); 188–189: IWM (E 1579); 190: IWM (HU 1205); 191: IWM (HU 39517); 192–193: IWM (A 4154); 194: Corbis/Hulton-Deutsch Collection; 196: IWM (HU 318); 197: IWM (HU 2283); 198–199: Corbis/Hulton-Deutsch Collection: 200: AKG-Images; 201: IWM (HU 39577); 202: Rodina Archive; 203: Rodina Archive; 204: Rodina Archive; 205: Rodina Archive; 206: IWM (NYF 22545); 207: IWM (HU 31329); 208: IWM (HU 2772); 209: IWM (OEM 1566); 210: IWM (AP 61595); 211: IWM (IND 885); 212: IWM (E 12919); 213: IWM (A 9115); 214: IWM (C 3186); 215: IWM (NY 13825); 216: IWM (HU 1808); 217: IWM (A 12835); 218–219: IWM (A 12661); 220: Rodina Archive; 221: IWM (MISC 54424); 222: Getty Images/Keystone; 223: AKG Images; 224: IWM (TR 1156); 225: Corbis/Bettmann; 226: IWM (NYF 14138); 228: (top) Rodina Archive; 229: (bottom) Rodina Archive; 231: Corbis/Hulton-Deutsch Collection; 232: IWM (NA 7748); 233: IWM (MH 1984); 234–235: Corbis; 236–237: Corbis; 238: Walter Frentz Historical Photo Archive; 239: IWM (E MOS 1451); 240: Getty Images/Fox Photos; 242: IWM (MH 2076); 243: (top) IWM (AP 25726); 243: (bottom) IWM (MH 4505); 244: Getty Images/Hulton Archive; 246: Getty Images/Keystone; 248: IWM (EA 31701); 249: IWM (HU 66477); 250: IWM (CH 16280); 251: IWM (D 21213); 252: (top) IWM (MH 2111B); 252: (bottom) IWM (TR 1386); 254: Corbis; 256: IWM (NYF 47538); 257: IWM (CP 51763); 258: BU 1163; 259: IWM (EA 47958); 260: U.S. National Archives & Records Administration; 261: IWM (EA 56685); 262: IWM (HU 68178); 263: IWM (OWIL 64545); 264: IWM (FRA 105752); 265: IWM (EA 62972); 266: IWM (NYP 80747); 267: IWM (NYP 59700); 268: Corbis/Bettmann; 270: Corbis/John Van Hasselt; 271: IWM (A 30426); 272: Corbis/Alinari Archives; 274: Corbis/Bettmann; 275: Getty Images/AFP; 276: Rex Features/Sipa; 277: Getty Images/Charles Hewitt; 278–279: Corbis/Hulton-Deutsch Collection; 280–281: Corbis/Bettmann; 282: Corbis/Hulton-Deutsch Collection; 283: Corbis/Hulton-Deutsch Collection: 284–285: Corbis/Bettmann; 286: Getty Images/Central Press; 287: © Magnum Photos Ltd./Raymond Depardon; 288: Getty Images/Robert Nickelsberg; 289: Corbis/Hulton-Deutsch Collection; 290–291: Getty Images/Bert Hardy; 292: Photos12.com/Bertelsmann Lexikon Verlag; 293: (top) Getty Images/Hank Walker/Time Life Pictures, (bottom) Getty Images/Bert Hardy; 294: Getty Images/And Romanowski Strickland/US Army/Time Life Pictures; 295. Getty Images/Bert Hardy; 296: Corbis/Bettmann; 297: Getty Images/Hulton Archive; 298: Corbis/Bettmann; 299: Getty Images/Miguel Vinas; 300: © Josef Koudelka / Magnum Photos; 301; Corbis/Bettmann; 302–303: Getty Images/Larry Burrows/Time Life Pictures; 304: Getty Images/Larry Burrows/Time Life Pictures; 305: Corbis/Bettmann; 306: Getty Images/Larry Burrows/Time Life Pictures; 307: Getty Images/Paul Schutzer/Time Life Pictures; 307: Getty Images/Larry Burrows/Time Life Pictures; 308–311: Getty Images/Larry Burrows/Time Life Pictures; 312–313: Corbis/Bettmann; 314: Topfoto.co.uk; 315–316: Getty Images/Larry Burrows/Time Life Pictures; 317: Getty Images/MPI; 318: Associated Press/Eddie Adams; 319: Corbis/Bettmann; 320: Corbis/Bettmann; 321: Corbis/Bettmann; 322: Corbis/Bettmann; 323: Getty Images/John Filo; 324–329: Corbis/Bettmann; 330: Associated Press/Nick Ut; 331–332: Corbis/Bettmann; 333: Corbis/Chris Rainier; 334–335: Corbis/Bettmann; 336: Corbis/Francoise de Mulder; 337: Corbis/Bettmann; 338–339: Getty Images/Scott Peterson; 340: Corbis/Jerry Cooke; 341: Corbis/Bettmann; 342: Corbis/Hulton-Deutsch Collection; 343: Corbis/Hulton-Deutsch Collection; 344: Corbis/Bettmann; 345: Corbis/Hulton-Deutsch Collection; 346–347: Corbis/Hulton-Deutsch Collection; 348: Corbis/Christian Simonpietri; 349: Rex Features/Sipa Press; 350: Corbis/Jacques Pavlovsky; 351: Getty Images/Roland Nevu; 352–353: Corbis/Bettmann; 354: Corbis/Reuters; 355: Getty Images/Robert Nickelsberg; 356: Cprbis/Reuters; 357: Getty Images/Joe China/U.S. Navy/Time Life Pictures; 358–359: Corbis/Geoff Lee/The Military Picture Library; 360: Corbis; 361: Getty Images/Anthony Suau; 362–363: Rex Features/Sipa Press; 364: Rex Features/Sipa Press; 365: Getty Images/Joe Raedle; 366–367: Corbis/Olivier Coret-Antoine Serra/In Visu; 368: Rex Features/Sipa Press; 369: Getty Images/ Curtis G. Hargrave/U.S. Army; 370–371: Getty Images/Central Press; 372: Getty Images/Keystone; 373: Corbis/Robert Patrick; 374: IWM (FKD 002028); 375: Corbis/John Hoagland; 376: Corbis/Reuters/Anibal Solimano; 377: Corbis/Bill Gentile; 378: Corbis/Eduardo Munoz/Reuters; 379: Corbis/Peter Turnley; 380: Getty/ Alexander Nemenov/AFP; 381: Rex Features/Sipa Press; 382: Emmanuel Ortiz & Patrick Chauvel/CORBIS; 383: Rex Features; 384–385: Corbis/Reuters; 386: Corbis/ Leif Skoogfors; 387: Corbis/Reuters/Oleg Popov; 388: Getty Images/ Said Khatib/AFP; 389: Getty Images/AFP; 390: Getty Images/U.S. Navy; 391: VIII/ James Nachtwey; 392: Corbis/Lynsey Addario; 393: Corbis/Reuters; 394: Getty Images/NVT/AFP; 395: Corbis/Stephanie Sinclair 396: Corbis/Kai Pfaffenbach/Reuters; 397: Corbis/Sergei Karpukhin/Reuters

Every effort has been made to acknowledge correctly and contact the source and/or copyright holder of each picture, and Carlton Books apologizes for any unintentional errors or omissions, which will be corrected in future editions of this book.